T0380662

Living philosophy

Righteous Soul, Real living

Seong Ju Choi

AuthorHouse™
1663 Liberty Drive
Bloomington, IN 47403
www.authorhouse.com
Phone: 1 (800) 839-8640

Because of the dynamic nature of the Internet, any web addresses or links contained in this book may have changed
since publication and may no longer be valid. The views expressed in this work are solely those of the author and do not
necessarily reflect the views of the publisher, and the publisher hereby disclaims any responsibility for them.

This book is printed on acid-free paper.

ISBN: 978-1-7283-2971-0 (sc)
ISBN: 978-1-7283-2972-7 (e)

Print information available on the last page.

Published by AuthorHouse 09/30/2019

authorHOUSE®

Living philosophy;

Righteous Soul, Real living

Seongju Choi / monk water

How to do "righteous soul, real living" the answer is clear

Problems also clear, problems is wicked soul macro concept world living purpose is "chance to be righteous soul" but it possible is only righteous soul mission carriage of "make lover righteous soul and bring back to the righteous soul living in destination place"

How to do "righteous soul, real living" is "share time with wicked soul, helps wicked soul, but also doing real love wicked soul" to save wicked soul to make righteous soul, this is real living.

Righteous soul, real living is

Righteous soul living going up of hard time, being "enlighten" and suffer of loss of going down being "nothing" then, the way of "the poor & righteous soul" in the end "righteous soul & nothing" so that righteous soul living running to the righteous soul living in destination place, safe returning to the righteous soul living in destination place.

2017.10.20; 3:47, toilet room hit me so, this is hearing broadcasting from Righteous soul living in destination place.

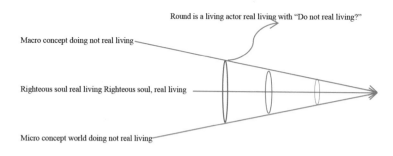

Round is a living actor real living with "Do not real living?"

Macro concept doing not real living

Righteous soul real living Righteous soul, real living

Micro concept world doing not real living

I want to tell "Righteous soul, Real living" this book, there is no define type, but this is must be concept book.

I will not say this is all actors are to be agreed, but I will write at least living righteous soul me, then I'm really being safe returning to the righteous soul living in destination place. This book will be confused because this is book or not, I will try to depend on my hearing broadcasting from righteous soul living in destination place.

This book main actor is Righteous soul "ME", so that I will write I'm a righteous soul, so that I'm running to the righteous soul living in destination place, while my experiment is written in this book. It must be it must be "concept only" not theory so that who read this book does not feel tension but just read book to end of pages.

Please write "me" to end of pages, and then all is helped from righteous soul living actor who living in macro concept world and micro concept world. Pure I'm depending on righteous souls talking to me through micro concept tunnel. These all basic knowledge from my 8 books; "micro concept", "excitement", "Love Engineering" "novel righteous soul "Me", "poem righteous soul", "poem water" "Righteous soul living and creature" "The poor righteous soul", I will depend on these books knowledges.

This book all be writing by the time series so that, I will all do record of year, month, day. This book can make me much more deeper living of righteous soul living. This book is not novel, but also philosophic book also; this book is creature of knowledge from righteous soul living in destination place through micro concept tunnel.

Who has been lived righteous soul living? How to live is righteous soul living?

Righteous soul "ME" want to explain by figuring of speech, then water flow down to the sea.

Water is righteous soul living actor

Running obstacles are wicked soul, mind level living actors.

3

Water living is running to the lower place, to the river run to destination place the sea.

Running water hit rock, stone, pebble, and water living plant, but also dead tree branches, even garbage and polluted trash, but all Water runs over the obstacles, water runs to the sea water.

Truly righteous soul is an actor, not a group, society, nation etc. this is not science but this is just living. So that real living of righteous soul living is same as water running to the sea water.

Rich, famous, success, living actor of macro concept world, then it must be expected from macro concept world, but that is not related with righteous soul of real living.

Running water just run to the have been destination place of the sea water. Running water help farmer to farming well, Running water offer fishes living place, running water to be seen beauty to macro concept living actors.

But running water is so hardly keep running down to the lowest place silently.

Here rock, stone, pebble, and water living plant, but also dead tree branches, even garbage and polluted trash is role of wicked soul, mind level living actor to the righteous soul living actor runs to the righteous soul living in destination place.

So why running to the righteous soul living actor behavior is the same as water behavior help farming, fish living place, but also good scenery to the macro concept world living actors.

So that righteous soul living actor keeps running to the righteous soul living in destination place, this is righteous soul living behavior "it shared time with other, help other but also doing real love others"

In the macro concept world living, real living of righteous soul living actor is must be mind is 1/, so long all endure of hard living of a righteous soul living.

A living actor only know who I am living in righteous soul living or not, so that actually no one know what I am living in righteous soul living.

This book "righteous soul, real living" protagonist is "righteous soul "ME", I am leading this book, so that I am a righteous soul living actor. Righteous soul me is still running to the righteous soul living in destination place, so that I am living in real living is try to do "it share time with other, help other, but also doing real love other".

as living Righteous soul living is conflict wicked soul living actor, but also mind level living actor, because they are doing not know righteous soul living way, so that their attitude is "easy living" "getting much more than others" so that all of produce macro concept world all criteria is for the wicked soul, and mind level living actor only, because macro concept world living actor do not know righteous soul living actor world.

righteous soul, real living is in the macro concept world saying "enlighten" similar living but micro concept world righteous soul living is of righteous soul living is safe returning to the righteous soul living in destination place where start to travel to the macro concept world.

so then, righteous soul "ME", I'm not excitement all of macro concept world living produce story, drama movie all, because these excitement contents are "revenge and break" of wicked soul living actor behavior is excitement, but also easy living of gambling, night drinking etc. but also mind level living actor jealous of "getting much more than other" so that anger and hate all of these contents for not me of righteous soul living "ME".

"Righteous soul "ME" in excitement is meditation; mind=1/, being the poor & righteous soul living, and righteous soul and nothing, this is real excitement to me.

"Righteous soul "ME" is living of real living, this is only in me, and truly I'm not social and economic success living actor. Truly it must be poor living must be. I'm a normal living actor, this is better to me; my prime concerning living is keeping running to the righteous soul living in destination place.

Righteous soul "ME" I'm tried to write this book, as hearing broadcasting from righteous soul living in destination place. So that this book is not same macro concept world criteria, this book mix philosophical but essay etc.

This book keep consistence in Righteous soul is actor, how to live is real living, if concentration then righteous soul "ME" how to my living is being righteous soul living of real living. I'm scare of out of me, because soul living world experiment is "me" also.

All of book is out from experiment "ME", this is point of macro concept world, truly macro concept world me watch me direction but also micro concept world direction me is writing tunnel, this realized from book "micro concept" writing, in addition that this book basic knowledge is derived from what I have written books knowledge.

Typically micro concept world direction is hearing broadcasting from righteous soul living in destination place, this broadcasting is to help running to the righteous soul living actor not to be out of road, but also how to overcome of macro concept world living with wicked soul living actor and mind level living actors.

When I'm writing book then I feel certify what I'm living in righteous soul living.

Righteous soul, Real living a day

A day living?

Arise in the morning is then changing body from lied down to get up.

But this is also resurrection from dead.

Start in the morning then new body from end of the day, but it also being of birth from righteous soul living in destination place

A day living is beginning "resurrection" "birth" this is start macro concept world living actor.

Righteous soul living actor feeling "resurrection" and "birth" as really excitement, because righteous soul have been dreamed to live righteous soul with body seeing feel of body living in excitement.

wicked soul living actor feeling "resurrection" and "birth" as being living easy living using " revenge and break" power.

truly macro concept world living actor living as "righteous soul" "wicked soul", righteous soul living in the micro concept place, so that watch out "thinking of wicked soul", then righteous soul living, but losing watching "thinking of wicked soul" then the living is in the wicked soul living.

Righteous soul "arise" "start" then living a day, this is meaning also "growing a day" this is righteous soul running to the righteous soul living in destination place.

"Growing a day" is real living. Truly macro concept living actor "growing a day" is physical living, but micro concept world living righteous soul is running to the righteous soul living in destination place, a day time and space is moved from not to the righteous soul living in destination place.

"Running to the righteous soul living in destination place" is understand as "enlighten" so "growing a day" is being righteous soul living these growing "from the poor & righteous soul to righteous soul & nothing" so long "growing a day" is real living.

"Growing a day is real living" is coming out, topic of this book "righteous soul, real living".

So then "arise" "start" "growing a day" then it is real living.

"Arise" is resurrection from dead, "start from the end" all is giving in righteous soul living again, how important and valuable living.

So that resurrected righteous soul living actor run for righteous soul living in destination place, this is so urgent. This is 'growing a day".

Macro concept living actor of righteous soul living actor "ME" feeling is "running for the righteous soul living in destination place" so that time and space is micro concept speed of "-1/~+1/".

righteous soul living actor live in the micro concept time and space"-1/~+1/" so that Righteous soul runs so past just like micro concept time and space, this is understand of macro concept living actors then "every moment is changed".

Righteous soul "ME" feeling is yes every moment is not changed all is new; it means that righteous soul living me is runs for the righteous soul living in destination place.

So that righteous soul "ME" how urgent to live in righteous soul "ME" all of righteous soul living is must be living in righteous soul living behavior "it shared time with other, help other, but also doing real love other" this is righteous soul, real living.

if living as wicked soul living in the time and space "growing a day" then wicked soul living actor do not run to the righteous soul living in destination place, so then wicked soul living is not living "growing a day", so called in the macro concept world living actor saying" living has been waste".

If righteous soul living actor sleeping then, truly occupied all wicked soul, the living is "there is no growing a day". Wicked soul of do not growing then, this is not real living.

Righteous soul living actor real living

A day living

"Arise" "start" "grow a day" Then it comes "lie down" "finish"

"Arise" is resurrection

"Start" is birth

"Grow a day" is running to the righteous soul living in destination place

"Lie dawn" is dead

"Finish" is reach at the righteous soul living in destination place.

Righteous soul "ME" a day is must be "start" "grow a day" "finish" is safe returning to the righteous soul living in destination place.

This is righteous soul living actor a day living, truly it is not easy because in the macro concept world living is going with wicked soul living actor, mind level living actors so that so many ignorance living actors are doing behavior damage righteous soul living "ME", in the end how to survive as righteous soul living "ME" is so urgent.

truly I was so hard to sleep in peace, in the time of sleeping so many temptation of wicked soul is cut in to righteous soul living "ME", this is so hard to live in righteous soul living me, it must be, in moment to safe returning time, changed into wicked soul living, so for the purpose of safe returning so it required to some safe tools.

I have been deep problems to me, so that righteous soul "ME" must be living "meditation ceremony is required" so righteous soul "ME" do live in every sleeping time I will do "meditation ceremony" then righteous soul "ME" safe reach at the righteous soul living in destination place.

This living is really righteous soul true living; this living is create excitement and helping me getting creation of knowledge.

In the macro concept world, everyday living in this living righteous soul living actor sure safe returning to the righteous soul living in destination place, Righteous soul living "ME" living eternity in excitement.

Suffering, hard living does accept by me in excitement

Coming excitement does accept by me in excitement

Righteous soul "ME" living is running for safe reaching in Righteous soul living in destination.

Someone in the macro concept world living actor living is mind level living actor, or wicked soul living actor.

Mind level living actor moment decision is to get much more than others, so that around of mind level actor, must be suffered and do hard to righteous soul "ME"

Furthermore wicked soul living actor moment decision is to be "easy living" for this wicked soul living actor use "revenge and break" so that Righteous soul "ME" is being suffering and living hard.

Righteous soul "ME" keep running to the righteous soul living in destination place, how to do?

suffering, being hard living cause of mind level living actor, and wicked soul living, righteous soul living "ME" so hard in living torture living.

But Righteous soul "ME" behavior "it shared time with other, help other, but also doing real love other".

Righteous soul living actor do live overcoming of excitement while living in the suffering being hard living even torture then do live in excitement, all do endure of excitement, then do just small power, but keep living in righteous soul living behavior "it shared time with other, help other, but also doing real love other".

In the end, Righteous soul "ME" feel in excitement, then do accept feeling in real excitement.

even small power of righteous soul living behavior, but it comes then it will comes to righteous soul living "ME" this righteous soul real living actor routine.

suffering, doing hard, torture of mind level, wicked soul, but if comes time to the righteous soul living "ME" excitement sure comes then feel excitement, this excitement is strong energy of righteous soul, so that running to the righteous soul living in destination place is going faster than time of suffering, doing hard, and torture of time.

Suffering, hard living does accept by me in excitement

Coming excitement does accept by me in excitement

This is macro concept world real living.

but truly righteous soul "ME" living actor also it is really do not live like "Suffering, hard living does accept by me in excitement" but Righteous soul "ME" is complain, anger to the mind level living actor and wicked soul living actor.

Then mind level living actor reply to righteous soul "ME"

mind level actor feeling, " I'm living to get much more than other, this is to be living well in the future" why this behavior is making hard righteous soul "ME", it never do not understand to mind level living actor.

Wicked soul living actor feeling "I'm living easy living" to do that I have to do "revenge and break", it never do not understand to wicked soul living actors.

Righteous soul "ME" under hard living, suffering but also torture living, then accept all these difficulties with excitement, do not anger to the wicked soul, mind level living actors.

This living is righteous soul, real living, this living is deep living, and this living is value and safe living from wicked soul living actor revenge, so that righteous soul "ME" living survive, but in the end reach at the righteous soul living in destination place.

Righteous soul "ME" empty me of wicked soul, furthermore all of macro concept living actor of wicked soul, and all empty from me.

To live in righteous soul, righteous soul "ME" followed mind=1/, and being the poor & righteous soul, in the end righteous soul & nothing.

so that Righteous soul "me" living in righteous soul, but this is not perfect righteous soul, because living in righteous soul "ME", so that I decide that righteous soul "ME" discard wicked soul but truly discard other is my first time, but righteous soul "ME" hard, torture from wicked soul so that I decide discard from me.

Furthermore I decide all of wicked soul others be discarded from me.

I will keep doing meditation, sometimes lazy before sleeping, but all of the day wicked soul trace all to be erase, today all of wicked soul trace must be cleaning from me, even much more erase trace all, then safe returning a day coming to the righteous soul living in destination place.

Righteous soul, real living and Righteous soul "ME" empty me of wicked soul

Truly already empty me this is all of other wicked soul also erased, but also my living of wicked soul is erased.

This is has been possible in me, but today I decide wicked soul also be emptied, furthermore all of wicked soul living actor also be empty from me.

Today what I have been learned righteous soul "ME" is keeping discarding, keep empty is righteous soul living and real living.

On today morning, I did all of communication tools are erased from my mobile phone.

What I feel in righteous soul but all trouble feeling because wicked soul trace is living in the righteous soul "ME" so that I decide it must be discarded from me that my wicked soul.

in me righteous soul, truly all discard even righteous soul also, because righteous soul create wicked soul, so that in me perfect being empty is being "nothing".

"Nothing" in me is real righteous soul "ME", nothing in me is righteous soul but also doing real living.

"Nothing in me" is there is no righteous soul also, just nothing, this is nothing and righteous soul is come true.

Righteous soul, real living is "Nothing in me" so then what is real living is keep erase and dis card wicked souls. This is real living.

Righteous soul "ME" real living is keeping discarding wicked soul trace from me, all of macro concept world living actor of wicked soul every moment all be cleaned discard from me.

Righteous soul, real living is running to the righteous soul living in destination place, doing righteous soul behavior "it shard time with other, help other, and doing real love other"

But also added "Righteous soul ME" be empty me of wicked soul.

If "empty in me" then it must be out of unsafe and fear, in the end reach at perfect peace in me, so it goes fast running to the righteous soul living in destination place.

If "empty me" then righteous soul "ME" run travel to far distance, so that righteous soul "ME" goes deep place. Righteous soul "ME" travel distance is width=1/, depth=, this is width multiply depth, 1/ multiply equal to 1.

In this righteous soul "ME" living do not make hard, suffer and torture, because width is conflict to others, so that to be make less in the end width=1/, running to the righteous soul living in destination place is going depth=.

So that righteous soul "ME" living is running to the deepest place of righteous soul living in destination place, this is also righteous soul, real living.

Righteous soul "ME" keep discarding, and erase all other wicked soul trace perfectly.

Righteous soul living "ME" is discarding wicked soul "ME", but also erase of wicked soul of son and daughter.

Then righteous soul living real living, this righteous soul real living is keeping running to the righteous soul living in destination place, this is righteous soul living.

Do not real living

Out of rail to the righteous soul living in destination place

Do not meditation

Do living "easy living"

Do not real living directly righteous soul "ME" is dim

Slowly wicked soul is occupied me

As then occur to me righteous soul living place being begin deteriorate

As living wicked soul me produce variable problems.

so then righteous soul living "ME" awaken keep seeking get into the righteous soul living way, running to the righteous soul living in destination place is safe living.

Righteous soul, real living is so real peak value.

Truly Righteous soul living is must be accepted by God

If I go with righteous soul living god, then I can go living righteous soul living, in the righteous soul living in destination place, then the living is real living.

Righteous soul living "ME" meditation then the place all be discard, all do real love, then the time and space is "nothing", but now righteous soul "me" meditation is not long, but when I felt in peace this is running to the righteous soul living in destination place.

Strangely experiment is

I didn't attend church cause of my idle, Monday my going to the work place, first getting taxi using move to rail road station, the point, happened trouble, in me world, sea water waved, I recognized that this week challenged to me.

then it is now middle of week so, then living is not, originality Righteous soul "me" is decreased, so then I was meeting dinner, so there a macro concept world living actor has given me "easy living" way to make woman friend.

While righteous soul "ME" living in safe, living in righteous soul living, in this time important thing is why meeting macro concept world living actor who is living in wicked soul living.

Then righteous soul "ME" influence of wicked soul living power.

Righteous soul "ME" and wicked soul other meet, the place happened front line, but if I live safe living in the righteous soul "ME" then, it must not to meet wicked soul living actor.

Living all of time and space are segregate and connect, all of living is decision and doing finished, end another decision and doing, keep connected.

the connection is being discard all of the past residue, then lighter then running to the righteous soul living in destination place, so long, in the decision must be getting lighter, but also decision to do living in righteous soul living behavior "it shared time with other, help other, but also doing real love other"

all of living is real living is "keep discard residue of past do, then the place must be cleaned, so long Righteous soul "ME" be cleaned, the cleaned place living well righteous soul, but also be lighten so that the place is so silent, in the end hear broadcasting from righteous soul living in destination place, it created knowledge to help righteous soul living actor run to righteous soul living in destination place.

Righteous soul, real living is all of time and space is "discard all of past residue being cleaning and fresh the time and space but also doing righteous soul behavior" this is real living.

So long feeling in the macro concept world living,

Then to discard residue of past living, then digest, and do poop is real living, so that past residue is all discarded in righteous soul living, then righteous soul living do live in best clean place, do behavior of righteous soul living

"It shared time with other, help other, but also doing real love other"

This behavior is possible, if do not discard past residue then truly do not live righteous soul living, because past wicked soul living is survive so then in me "revenge and breaking other" is survive.

to live righteous soul living "ME" do real living, do righteous soul living behavior then it required to righteous soul "ME" discard past residue, this is very required to live in righteous soul living.

Righteous soul, real living is keep discarding past residue and does righteous soul living behavior this is keep routine is real living.

past residue is infer that all of wicked soul, behavior, mind level living behavior poop, but righteous soul living behavior past also changed into wicked soul past residue of poop, so that it required all of past residue poop discarded.

Why I'm hard?

I was temptation from wicked soul last night. The temptation is body related thing.

Truly I was in the fog in me, not clear, with feeling of lonely; this is lead me to the trap in the temptation from wicked soul.

As deep resting was weekend, but start a new place of work place, righteous soul "ME" is living in weekend living, because I'm working at the 2.5 hours of distance from home.

Home living not in peace, but sleep peace, but out of home is peace in the macro concept world, but sleep in not easy, right before sleeping; I'm usually being temptation from wicked soul.

Therefore now, my feeling is not clear but feeling guilty. Yes I'm in the prison now. at the time of macro to micro, this is sleeping, but it must be a day being end, but begin a night, here is life scale then, must be disappeared from macro concept world.

In me, it directs me to do something, this is writing. Righteous soul "ME", in me also there is not living in righteous soul living, then how to live out of me, in me the place also a wicked soul and righteous soul living actor coincident living, but how to do, in the macro concept world.

by the way, at now seen of macro concept world all is derived from "thinking of wicked soul" so then, macro concept world is truly" thinking of wicked soul" but also macro concept world is "thinking of wicked soul and mind living of getting much more than other" this is macro concept world living.

My macro concept world living is 3days living in home, four days out of home, living criteria is home and out of home. in the micro concept world living also must be home and out of home.

In home is must be living in the righteous soul living in destination place, but out of home is wicked soul living in destination place. because of in home is " it share time with other, help other, but also doing real love other" is going well, but out of home is broken righteous soul living.

I didn't recognized that but it is concept of that, macro concept world family is keep in micro concept world living, so that if do not live in righteous soul living then, a living actor who live in wicked soul then, the actor do not live with righteous soul of family living actors.

righteous soul living is keep doing in the family, so then how important it is, I did not know, why it share time with other, is family living is very important to live my time with family, this is basic, after then help family, and do real love family.

Why god create family, on today learned and realized.

Until now, righteous soul and family, I didn't know, but my righteous soul living actor, living with other, here other is family.

wicked soul do not know, family, so that even living in family, all of family living still a wicked soul keep "easy living" but also, in the family " wicked soul do not shared time with family, but also do not help family but also do not real love family" then wicked soul living actor, just feel personal easy living.

actually righteous soul "ME" as possible as can do not living out of righteous soul "ME" but dare today saying comes; a living of wicked soul is personal easy living, so that, wicked soul living actor conflict in home, wicked soul living "easy living" actor do energy "revenge and break" strong, so that wicked soul living actor break family.

Wicked soul do not know righteous soul living behavior "it shared time with other, help other, but also doing real love other", this is living of righteous soul living, Righteous soul living behavior not me but other, then this chain is feedback then Righteous soul "ME" living be shared other time, and other help me, but also other do real love me.

This is real living, this is righteous soul living, righteous soul and family, this is comes to righteous soul "ME", Righteous soul living is family living.

truly, righteous soul "ME" 3days home, 4 days out of home, then three days living in righteous soul living of real living.

My wife is tried to share living. She has her job, for long time 27 years, my job has been done same, "we shared time with other, help other, but also doing real love other".

Righteous soul "ME" also source of product, personal living, this is dong not living usually, so that my living also responsibility making living in personal living.

but righteous soul "ME", this is challenge to me, this is so kinship, so that this is if wicked soul power so huge then, I will be must be target from wicked soul to revenge and break, then it must be disappeared.

For me living is perfectly shared time with other, help other, but also do real love other", that that all

if Righteous soul "ME" huge strong, then I can do " I will shared time with my wife, help my wife, and doing real love wife"

What is righteous soul, real living?

This answer is simple, righteous soul real living, then safe return to the righteous soul living in destination place.

Here is my Righteous soul "ME", how to live as righteous soul, real living.

At first, recognition of who and what I am

Here is macro concept world and micro concept world

Macro concept world begin is birth

Micro concept world begin is dead of macro concept world.

Macro concept world is seen world

Micro concept world is unseen world

Righteous soul living "ME" is both macro concept world and micro concept world.

But mind level living actor world is only macro concept world of seen world.

If mind level living actor is 1/, then it appeared of recognition of righteous soul "ME" and wicked soul "ME".

As result of mind is disappearing from me then it must be appeared soul living, in this time of seen world is soul is living in the body. so that even though mind is 1/ then sure of soul living, but soul is not seen to any actors.

But in the soul room, righteous soul and wicked soul is living.

Macro concept world living place all of living actors are living, such as wicked soul, righteous soul, mind level living actors.

Birth is macro concept world beginning

Dead is micro concept world beginning?

Macro concept world is mixing place; wicked soul, righteous soul, mind level living actor

But micro concept world living place is divided as righteous soul living in destination place from wicked soul living in destination place.

Dead of macro concept world, then righteous soul living in destination place; only righteous soul living, so that express as righteous soul living actor safe returned to the home of righteous soul living in destination place.

Another dead of macro concept world, then wicked soul living in destination place, out of righteous soul living actors are all living in the micro concept world. In micro concept world wicked soul living in destination place are living such as wicked soul, mind level living actors.

Righteous soul living "me" how to safe returning to the righteous soul living in destination place, this is righteous soul, real living.

Righteous soul living "ME" structure changed as near to the righteous soul living in destination place.

Righteous soul living "ME" is running from birth to safe returning to the righteous soul living in destination place.

this is righteous soul living "ME" traveling from righteous soul living in destination place via micro concept world to macro concept world then safe returning to righteous soul living in destination place.

Righteous soul, real living

Real living is all related with running to the righteous soul living in destination place, how to do?

Righteous soul living actor first survives living among wicked soul, righteous soul, and mind level living actors in the macro concept world.

Survive righteous soul structure is "wicked soul, righteous soul + mind + body"

Righteous soul living actor in the macro concept world living time is not endless, so that during living in macro concept world, survive and doing living righteous soul living behavior; "it shared time with others, help others, but also do real love other"

truly righteous soul living actor running to the righteous soul living in destination place, practice how to live in righteous soul living in destination place, in the righteous soul living in destination place living is "it shared time with others, help others, but also do real love other"

So that righteous soul living actor do real living is?

real living is righteous soul living behavior "it shared time with others, help others, but also do real love other" this is real living.

Righteous soul "ME" structure is changed just like

Birth; (wicked soul, righteous soul) + mind + body

As living righteous soul, righteous soul recognition then

(Wicked soul, righteous soul) + Mind=1/ + body

As keep growing then (Wicked soul, righteous soul) + body

here is righteous soul must be survived from wicked soul, how to live righteous soul living actor, it must be wicked soul is "easy living" to live, use "revenge and break" so that righteous soul living actor do live in hard living, so that righteous soul living is being "the poor & righteous soul" and "righteous soul & nothing".

survived of "the poor & righteous soul" and "righteous soul & nothing" in the end if dead then structure is

Survived righteous soul of righteous soul & nothing + body= this actor is macro concept world living, this is righteous soul without wicked soul, so that any wicked soul do not harm to the wicked soul, so long, righteous soul & nothing be righteous soul, it already segregated from wicked soul, so that in the macro concept world righteous soul living actor living in safe.

As macro concept world dead then structure is

Righteous soul & nothing + body; disappeared from macro concept world" = Righteous soul

At now, Righteous soul is begin is micro concept world, safe returning to the micro concept world righteous soul living in destination place.

As result of macro concept world righteous soul "ME" keep discard from righteous soul, this is real living.

Righteous soul "ME" is keep discarding wicked soul "ME", mind level "ME" all make garbage then in the end, /righteous soul is only survive.

Righteous soul, Real living is actual living "ME" I will live in righteous soul living.

Why try to write this book, "righteous soul, real living"

living is so hurry to make money, not to be lose making money all of time is consumed for this only, so then it must be safe living, but this is real living, if real living is righteous what is righteous soul living.

What are problems?

If living righteous soul, real living then, it must be there is no wicked soul and not real living.

if live in righteous soul, real living then it must be safe living and returning to the righteous soul living in destination place, it must be around of me all of living actors are all safe living in righteous soul living in destination place.

But if living now actors do not know of "righteous soul, real living" then they living is all for making money.

To get much money is real living, but this living is not living of righteous soul living.

So that this book writing aim is to help try to live in righteous soul living but also how to live is real living, so this book is to do live in righteous soul and real living.

Eternity real living is "righteous soul living actor do real living so that this living running to the righteous soul living in destination place"

This is real living in the macro concept world.

Righteous soul, real living

Righteous soul; living in progress the poor & righteous soul, and righteous soul & nothing, so then around of righteous soul, wicked soul, mind level living actors but also another righteous soul living actor.

Righteous soul living actor behavior; "it shared time with others, help others, but also doing real love others"

if wicked soul, mind level living actors are only living to a righteous soul living actor, then as survive among them, it must be live "the poor & righteous soul living", this living is suffer, hard, poor living.

Real living; real living antonym is fake living, false living, so then real living with fake living, false living. But actually what is real living, what is not real living is not discriminate.

In the macro concept world living place, real living from false living is how to define. In this book, real living is doing "running to the righteous soul living in destination place", cannot running to the righteous soul living in destination place then truly do not real living.

Why in this book try to say "righteous soul, real living"

In the macro concept world living actor living in peace, living in excitement most living actors are wanted living.

Righteous soul living actor try to running to the righteous soul living in destination place, it keeps living peace and excitement living.

Strangely if I live other wicked soul living actor then, "righteous soul "ME" is influenced by the wicked soul living actor, and then my inside is also break peace and excitement.

Righteous soul, real living

It must be infer that if "righteous soul "ME" doing righteous soul, real living then, around of me, the other will be feel in peace and excitement.

Righteous soul living actor behavior itself is doing good influence other, but wicked soul living actor behavior itself is doing bad influenced.

good manner, bad manner make good other, make bad other, in this case, hard to defense from bad manner to bad influence me, this is automatically comes in, around wicked soul do harms automatically.

How to live in the macro concept world living, without being influenced from around wicked soul, mind level living actors, it must be living "water" water is keep running down to the place which ever block then go run around, without anger to the block something.

Water runs running over, running around, keeps running to the lowest place. Water will be stopped in the lowest place.

if righteous soul living actor is same as "water" then, righteous soul living "me" must be same as "water running" without any do harmed from around wicked soul, mind level living actors, then righteous soul living of water runs over the wicked soul, and mind level living actor, but also go around them also.

In the seen in the macro concept world all of living actor with water, so that water is helper of macro concept world living thing which are plants are animal all is needed water.

So that water helps other living, this is righteous soul living behavior "it shared time with other, help other, but also doing real love other" Righteous soul "ME" grown to now, so many righteous soul living actors are helped me. Living like me is not make me by myself, my growing is required someone helping me to grow.

water, Righteous soul, is all just do " it shared time with other, help other, but also doing real love other" because water is all is sacrifice to help and love, someone drink water, the roots absorb water, but water used up for living, but water still living, in the blood, in the tree sap.

Water living is not feel fear of drinking, absorbing, because water living in eternity. the same as righteous soul living is not fear because of righteous soul living running to the righteous soul living in destination living place, as righteous soul living eternity.

Righteous soul "Me" so many times I met righteous soul living actors who are real living of helping me, each time they all good manners; these righteous soul living behavior, make me now "righteous soul living "ME".

They are all living in water, just do all to me; truly they are all living of righteous soul living actors.

If a righteous soul living actor live is so hard, but a righteous soul living actor live hearing broadcasting from righteous soul living in destination place. The righteous soul living actor can get creation of knowledge, which is open for the new road to the righteous soul living in destination place.

it not anyone to live in righteous soul living, so that whoever all do not hearing broadcasting from righteous soul living in destination place, then no one know to build road to the righteous soul living in destination place. So then there is no any creation of knowledge.

I'm here writing, so then I'm so excitement to me, writing is my all of behavior, writing is real living to me, because without doing then, who can be peace and excitement, right before I was not written, if I try to write then, righteous soul "ME" feel in excitement.

Writing is communicating with righteous soul living actors through micro concept point; tunnel, when I'm writing then I met righteous soul living in destination place living actor who tries to help me.

My writing is all helped from righteous soul living in destination place living actors. Such as all living in righteous soul living in the macro concept world, they are all lived in righteous soul living, so that their time was so peace, in peace living the poor & righteous soul living was also excitement, because of other righteous soul living actor keep helping me to live on in the street beggar living like.

As I'm living in righteous soul living which not perfect righteous soul is living, but keep living in righteous soul living the show is I can hear broadcasting from righteous soul living in destination place.

Righteous soul, real living!

in the macro concept world living actors are living, if living in wicked soul living then, "easy living" is prime living, so that, to be easy living wicked soul living actor use energy "revenge and break energy", in macro concept world living who will live in wicked soul living, this is simple question, but truly it is not easy to answer.

If someone asks me question?

The question is who will live in "hard live" and "easy living" then this problem answer is not simple.

Hard living is philosophical righteous soul living, but easy living is philosophically wicked soul living, truly this is not showing, but hidden concept.

Most macro concept world living actors are all to be "easy living" select, truly I do, so that "hard living" itself is righteous soul living, because only "God" do real love who is living hard, because god is righteous soul living actor's king.

But some actor select living "hard" then it must be "hard living" also living in excitement is enlighten essential, so that hard living also so excitement compared with "easy living" what is feeling of hard living excitement? then hard living actor, all of time in hard so that it simple hard living, in the hard living excitement, then the actor there is no "easy living" actor, so that only hard living is only actor self.

'hard living" at now, Righteous soul "ME" hard live, is against to the "easy living", so that hard living is safe living from "easy living" but also "hard living" it required to be "hard living" problems solving so that "hard living" actor simple to be getting better, it must but, an actor choose living "hard" then, an actor "hard living" is usual, but to the easy living actor is so fear of "hard living".

"hard living"≠"easy living"

"Hard living" deep hard living = make sense

"Easy living" deep easy living = do not make sense

deep hard living create righteous soul using knowledge, creation of knowledge, it means that "deep hard living" as deep hard living actor running to the creation of knowledge creating place, in this book, righteous soul living in destination place

"Deep easy living" = do not make sense, become shallow, try to be deep, but there is no further deeper place in "deep easy living" because it already easy so that easy must be deeper easy is still easy. In this place, there is no produce to overcoming easy living, and then there is no creation of knowledge.

What is real living, who is real living, who is goes deeper, this is "hard living" but whoever do not want to be hard live.

But some actor live in "hard live" actively

then, active in "hard live" actor living in righteous soul living, in the end active in righteous soul living hearing broadcasting from righteous soul living in destination place.

"Hard live" righteous soul living behavior is survive from "wicked soul easy living" so then "hard live in righteous soul living, then "hard living" is distance from wicked soul, this moment, so righteous soul living actor safe from wicked soul, so that it is really excitement, so long, "hard living righteous soul" hear broadcasting from righteous soul living in destination place.

Righteous soul "hard living" to do with hearing broadcasting from righteous soul living in destination place, but also Righteous soul "hard living" bring creation of knowledge to this living for whom all of living of righteous soul living actors.

So then living in righteous soul living is for actor self, but a living of righteous soul living is for all of righteous soul living actor creation of knowledge creation is urgent working.

as living an righteous soul living, an righteous soul keep in touch with righteous soul living, so that righteous soul living god keep watching righteous soul, so that righteous soul living in destination place, do against to the wicked soul living in destination of king, so then it do not happened wicked soul living actor energy of "revenge and break power" so that cause of a righteous soul living, that the place is still living righteous soul living so that defend all of wicked soul living behavior.

Righteous soul, real living is just survive as righteous soul living, then it is keep peace from wicked soul breaking peace.

In conclusion then righteous soul living itself is real living, and then it runs to the righteous soul living in destination place.

As about to reach at the righteous soul living in destination place, it must be the righteous soul living actor being "righteous soul & nothing"

Here is "Nothing" is start from something. Something is start from nothing.

Macro concept living actor comes from righteous soul "nothing" to appeared in the macro concept world be being something.

Here is something is "righteous soul, wicked soul and mind with body" so that it beings that something.

From nothing to something then, getting body is excitement purpose. So that getting something of righteous soul to meet is really dreamed, in the living of righteous soul so not meet body cause of wicked soul and mind, then still righteous soul seek body, then it is still "something", so that in the macro concept world getting is permitted, but also getting to be something is kind of excitement living.

But after righteous soul meet body, then at now accomplishment righteous soul macro concept tour purpose, then righteous soul being "something" then this is matter of wicked soul's "revenge and break target" this means that macro concept of righteous soul living actor so dangerous survive, so that from now on, from something to "nothing" for the purpose of safe returning to the righteous soul living in destination place.

in the macro concept world, righteous soul meeting after body, then in apt to living in the body, so that it is real excitement, but in a moment, excitement righteous soul, also possible being disappeared from macro concept world living, in this also, "something" to "nothing" is so hard righteous soul living, but righteous soul living behavior is to be "righteous soul & nothing" it must be being "nothing" is required, this is righteous soul living running to the righteous soul living in destination place.

so fulfilment micro concept world righteous soul to meet body living excitement, then micro concept world living actor feel peak in excitement, but if the excitement longer then all of righteous soul living energy run out, then the place will occupied by wicked soul, so in the end righteous soul disappeared in the macro concept world, this means that, righteous soul living actor cannot safe returning to the righteous soul living in destination place.

So why being "Nothing" to "something" then it must be running to the" Nothing" of righteous soul & nothing.

In the macro concept world "nothing" is macro concept world structure is "being nothing"

"Something" = righteous soul, wicked soul, mind with body

"Nothing" = Righteous soul being nothing living in shelter of "body"

In the end of mind level as body is disappeared from righteous soul & nothing, then the time is safe returning to the righteous soul living in destination place.

How to live is in the macro concept world being "nothing" is "it shared time with other, help other, but also doing real love other" then all of something is being "nothing".

While righteous soul living in the macro concept world being excitement to being "nothing", this is righteous soul living in destination place reach at.

As being "nothing" then it must be disappeared all of wicked soul, and mind level living problems all being "nothing".

This is what I said before of righteous soul living actor running is "the poor & righteous soul living changed righteous soul & nothing"

"Nothing" is Unseen righteous soul.

"Nothing unseen righteous soul living" is must be living of old living in the macro concept world. This is righteous soul, real living.

Righteous soul, real living is as being old, then the righteous soul living be peace in living with excitement. This is natural, righteous soul living actor harvest is "peace and excitement".

If do not living in righteous soul living, then nothing to something in macro concept of living is still living in "something" then, this is must be expected "something in excitement micro concept world righteous soul" but if living in keep "something" then, the living must be attacked from wicked soul who has power of "revenge and break" so that, still something of righteous soul living actor being disappeared before harvest, before reach at the "righteous soul & nothing" so long, the righteous soul of something disappeared, it very unexpected thing is happened righteous soul so not safe returning to the righteous soul living in destination place.

Righteous soul "me" Righteous soul living behavior is "it shared time with other, help other, but also doing real love other"

Help other is also real living.

Last night surprisingly I did pray other structure change

wicked soul + righteous soul + mind + body to be righteous soul living it must be, mind is 1/, and cause of doing real love wicked soul, wicked soul to be changed into righteous soul, so that it must be equal to be= righteous soul + body= as body is being righteous soul living shelter so that it appeared up perfect righteous soul, righteous soul & nothing, in the end "nothing of living in righteous soul living in destination place"

righteous soul living "ME" help other, is must be making "righteous soul living" to help, so long, even I can't so perfectly make other righteous soul, but as what is do help to make righteous soul then, the wicked soul is helped from righteous soul "me", so that in the wicked soul of righteous soul living actor being helped from Righteous soul "me" strong righteous soul.

It is "righteous soul, real living"

"Righteous soul, real living is to help other being "righteous soul", this is real living.

this is must be "righteous soul "ME" also making strong not to be wicked soul "revenge and break" then survive from wicked soul and do "righteous soul behavior" " it shared time with other, help other, but also doing real love other".

Here is righteous soul "ME" real love other and help other, then it must be a wicked soul living actor be changed into being real love sunshine to other, so then this structure

Righteous soul move from righteous soul "me" from me to other to help other, so long do righteous soul living behavior "it shared time with other, help other, but also doing real love other"

so long Righteous soul me structure " righteous soul + body" then here is righteous soul behavior is "righteous soul can do real love" so then, righteous soul living actor do righteous soul behavior, so that other wicked soul is meet righteous soul "ME" so that if righteous soul meet other

"Righteous soul "ME" + wicked soul living actor" wicked soul, righteous soul +mind+ body"= "wicked soul + righteous soul "ME" doing real love+ righteous soul + mind + body"

=wicked soul + strong righteous soul doing real love+ weak righteous soul + mind + body= as keep doing righteous soul living behavior " it shared time with other, help other, then doing real love other" of righteous soul "ME" real living, in the end the wicked soul structure being changed in to being righteous soul living.

so long, = {wicked soul + strong righteous soul doing real love+ weak righteous soul} + mind + body= wicked soul being changed into righteous soul living, mind is being 1/, it means that mind can't use wicked soul " revenge and break energy" so that mind is being decreased to 1/, in the end as keep righteous soul living actor "ME" do righteous soul living behavior "it shared time other, help other, but also doing real love other", then, in the wicked soul structure must be changed

[{wicked soul + weak righteous soul} + strong righteous soul + real love] + mind=1/ + body", this is needed time to be whole living, if righteous soul "ME" is find lover, then the wicked soul lover, being changed keeping progress to be living in righteous soul living, so that whole living sacrifice to make lover to be changed into righteous soul living lover.

As strong righteous soul +real love is being =, then righteous soul "me" is being "righteous soul & nothing" so long, then it must be changed [{wicked soul + weak righteous soul} + strong righteous soul + real love] + mind=1/∞ + body = strong righteous soul + strong righteous soul +2 doing real love = 2 righteous soul & nothing. So long righteous soul "me" and lover of righteous soul is appeared into macro concept world, in the end, body of shelter is disappeared then, it appeared two righteous soul & nothing, in the end righteous soul living in destination place, safe reach in the end, there is all being "nothing" of righteous soul.

Righteous soul living behavior is "it shared time with other, help other, but also doing real love other"

righteous soul, real living is what I said before, but also, it must be being righteous soul living actor, if this living is real living, if my living is do not carry this, then this living is direction to go, to do.

just like me, try to be live in real living, then the living actor even lost road but until then it must be gat reach at the road to running to the righteous soul living in destination place.

Righteous soul living behavior of "doing real love other" is as macro concept world living actor all be gift using in the living of macro concept world living, this "doing real love other" had been gift from righteous soul living in destination place, a righteous soul who finished macro concept world safe, so the righteous soul living actor now perfect righteous soul, it don't have to turning back to the macro concept world tour to meet lover, because a righteous soul did clear of macro concept world voyage, a righteous soul had meet, then do righteous soul living behavior to the lover, then the love who had lived as wicked soul, but the lover changed into righteous soul living actor.

then lover also enlighten so that lover also remembered gift from righteous soul living in destination place, so that the lover mission is getting righteous soul of lover, then both righteous soul mission clear.

A righteous soul said the only way to safe returning to the righteous soul living in destination place, then do use "doing real love other".

Before move to tour, a righteous soul said repeat, "Do real love other" at that time it must be "I will do real love other"

Who knows that? doing "real love is not easy" because all of living actor in the macro concept world, all of living actor is forget but now living is just only mind level living actor of "getting much more than other" but also wicked soul living actors are all try to living "easy living using revenge and break energy". Wicked soul living is easily use wicked soul of energy "revenge and break".

"Doing real love"

righteous soul, real living is in the macro concept world is "righteous soul + body" then, this is truly real living, micro concept is there is no body, then how to live is real living.

righteous soul living in destination place, expect to live excitement in the righteous soul in the macro concept world, this is real living, but truly macro concept world living righteous soul living actor meet body, all come true of expect in the micro concept world.

Righteous soul real living

But truly macro concept world living all of living actors are living in same place

Wicked soul, righteous soul, mind level living actor,

But also,

Wicked soul structure is "wicked soul, righteous soul=1/+ (mind +body)

Righteous soul is "wicked soul=1/, righteous soul +(mind=1/ +body)

Mind level living actor "wicked soul? Righteous soul is? + (mind+ body)

These living actors are living in the macro concept world living.

So that righteous soul real living to be that how hard, so that safe returning righteous soul said "do use to survive in the macro concept world"

Righteous soul "doing real love other", if this living is so hard because most macro concept living actor try to live in "easy living" this is who dare condemn, because in the macro concept world living place, most living actor try to live "easy living".

righteous soul living behavior is real living, because righteous soul living behavior is keep same of circulation of macro concept world living righteous soul living actor survive, so that macro concept righteous soul do live same behavior as did in righteous soul living in destination place. So that righteous soul living in destination place is righteous soul living but also macro concept world righteous soul.

Macro concept world living place is an actor self-decision; living wicked soul, living righteous soul, living mind level living.

So then if wrong living so that wicked soul living then, it must be changed living to righteous soul living is decided in the macro concept world.

If a righteous soul mission clear to save lover from wicked soul to righteous soul, then a righteous soul living is "real living".

So that righteous soul living is real living because righteous soul living actor "it shared time with lover, help lover, and doing real love lover to be changed wicked soul lover to righteous soul lover".

Here is comes what is righteous soul real living

Answer is "save wicked soul living lover and make lover to make righteous soul living actor" this is real living.

Righteous soul, real living

Then naturally this living is same living of micro concept world, and macro concept world as living of righteous soul living actor and living righteous soul.

Righteous soul, real living

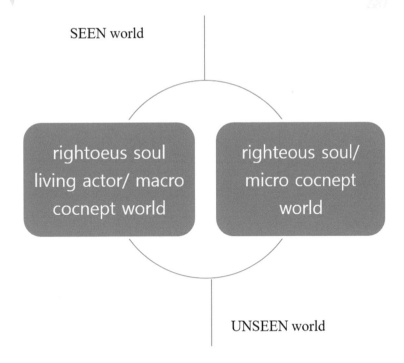

Righteous soul, real living is SEEN, UNSEEN world all living must be excitement, but truly macro concept world SEEN world, living is so hard to live survive from wicked soul, so then, segregated from wicked soul living, the place righteous soul living in destination is not wicked soul living, UNSEEN world living is only living righteous soul so that, the place being living in excitement.

UNSEEN world micro concept world of righteous soul still same as "it shared time with other, help other, but also doing real love other" here is other is macro concept world righteous soul living, who is need to solve problems to run to righteous soul living in destination place.

So that even UNSEEN world righteous soul connect through micro concept point {-1/~+1/} so that among righteous soul living actor to righteous soul meet through micro concept point, how to live is righteous soul, real living is required in the SEEN world.

Righteous soul real living is

"It shared time with other, help other, but also doing real love other"

Doing real love other

Until to now, other must be living actor, but love object expanded

"Loving other" is "loving space"

"Help other" is can help solving problems then "help other" is "creating = help, space"

Righteous soul living, real living is making other excitement

"It shared time with other, help other, but also doing real love other"

It behavior is must be other living actor, or space are all be excitement.

While try to living in righteous soul "Me" but I did not know, make other being excitement, then righteous soul "me" must be showing to other feel "excitement".

"Create space" originality created real living space, this is who create, must be righteous soul living actor god, this is the god creating.

Righteous soul, real living "creature space" is ultimate being making other "excitement".

In the living of macro concept world, righteous soul living actor is being helped from righteous soul living in destination place.

Righteous soul do real love space, then how to love, then righteous soul living actor through micro concept point, to meet how to love space, then it must be righteous soul living actor doing righteous soul living behavior "it shared time with other, help other, but also doing real love other" then, righteous soul living in destination place, righteous soul help how to "creating space", this is also doing real love.

Righteous soul, real living and "creature"

"Creature" is new living. whoever did not go living way, but righteous soul living actor living is "creative a new living" then, righteous soul living is running to the righteous soul living in destination place, so that the running voyage is all of direction and road to be not lost, keep hearing broadcasting from righteous soul living in destination place.

Righteous souls "ME" running to the righteous soul living in destination place, how to come to me, make me hearing broadcasting.

Righteous soul living running to the righteous soul living actor, must run to the righteous soul living.

Righteous soul living actor helped from righteous soul living, so that macro concept world righteous soul living "ME" sometimes hard, after hard reach at the place of righteous soul living go by way of area, but this righteous soul living running is new and creature.

"new and creature" all the time find but also decision is required, but also solve the problems this is keep running righteous soul living actor behavior.

who can help righteous soul living actor run to righteous soul living in destination place, this is all from righteous soul living in destination place, righteous soul, real living is the place is mind=1/, but also "the poor & righteous soul living" in the end of righteous soul living is "righteous soul & nothing".

Who knows righteous soul living "the poor & righteous soul" so long, in the living of righteous soul living is at first mind=1/, then find the micro concept point (-1/~+1/, and then it appeared righteous soul living actor "the poor & righteous soul living actor" who knows that how hard to live poor living, even micro concept point of view, righteous soul "me" is righteous soul living actor running, but macro concept world living "me" is truly poor.

"The Poor living" how hard living, just righteous soul real living is required to live in poor.

"Creature of righteous soul living" is real living.

Real living is creature, so then try and error also happened to live as righteous soul living.

"Creature of righteous soul living space" is real living, that is connected with righteous soul living. Macro concept world living space is how to do, is also the macro concept world space is being is the running to the righteous soul living, and then if the space is creation of new, the space is running to the righteous soul living in destination place.

Creation of space is doing by the righteous soul living in destination place god helping is appeared as creation of knowledge.

Righteous soul, creation of space is real living

If space occupation is not by righteous soul then, the place is wicked soul living actor living place only, without creation of space.

Without doing occupation space would be running to the wicked soul living in destination place. this place is "easy living" without creature of living actor, so called the actor is wicked soul living actor, wicked soul living actor do not know creature.

Creation space is righteous soul living actor place, ultimate righteous soul living actor reach at the excitement.

Righteous soul "me" is "sunshine" so that Righteous soul living itself is automatically doing righteous soul, real living "it shared time with other, help other, but also doing real love other".

what I'm real living righteous soul living "ME" then in me being "sunshine" please righteous soul "ME" being bright "sunshine".

Righteous soul, real living is righteous soul "ME" living in truth.

Righteous soul living is hearing broadcasting from righteous soul living in destination place.

Hearing broadcasting is creation of knowledge which is to help running to the righteous soul living in destination place.

Creation of knowledge is truth.

True of creation knowledge, it is real living.

True of creation knowledge is same as righteous soul living.

Righteous soul living "me" is true of creation knowledge.

Living righteous soul "ME" feeling true of creation of knowledge through micro concept gate (-1/~+1/), every time and moment hearing broadcasting from righteous soul living in destination place, so that righteous soul "me" live whole true of creation knowledge.

Righteous soul, it does real living

Wicked soul, it does not real living.

Righteous soul, it does real living

Real living is recognition from righteous soul living in destination place.

Not real living is not recognition from righteous soul living in destination place

Macro concept world living mind level living actor

these living actors are living doing now recognition righteous soul, wicked soul but only living "mind + body" so that mindful body, do not know righteous soul, wicked soul, so long, macro concept world mind level living actor is do not know micro concept world living.

So then mind level living actor if enlighten then the actor be "Righteous soul, it does real living" if not to be "Wicked soul, it does not real living"

Righteous soul, it does real living

Wicked soul, it does not real living.

enlighten righteous soul, it does real living is recognition from righteous soul living in destination place, so that righteous soul living of living time run to the righteous soul living in destination place, but if moment do not live righteous soul living then, the living is not real living, so that even used time but at that moment is do not running to the righteous soul living in destination place.

Righteous soul, it does real living is value to be suffer, hard, difficult living, because this living has been certified to be living in the righteous soul living in destination place.

Righteous soul, real living actor how to say: voice then it must be righteous soul saying then, the saying also sound from righteous soul living in destination place.

Righteous soul living in destination place living righteous soul how to say, this must be "righteous soul sound, saying of original from righteous soul living in destination place"

Righteous soul living actor saying is from righteous soul living in destination place is creature of knowledge is saying. just communicating with righteous soul living sound without wake wicked soul up, righteous soul living actor saying is " righteous soul saying from righteous soul living in destination place" this voice make other be feeling warm feeling, real loving feeling.

If out of righteous soul saying, then it must be other also "it will be sleeping wicked soul will be awaken" so that righteous soul living actor peace will be broken.

righteous soul living actor saying is "until wicked soul is not awaken but saying righteous soul living, so that righteous soul saying without awaken wicked soul, then the time saying is righteous soul living actor to actor meeting and talking, this time righteous soul saying is through micro concept point, tunnel to reach at the other of righteous soul living actor, so that, the righteous soul living actor saying is all being "righteous soul living actor of creation of knowledge transfer to the other righteous soul living actors.

as saying righteous soul living actor saying give real love to other, so that righteous soul living actor saying is just speaker of broadcasting from righteous soul living in destination place.

righteous soul living in destination place broadcasting all help righteous soul living actor safe running to the righteous soul living in destination place, here is hearing from broadcasting communicate using righteous soul living saying to other righteous soul living actors to help running to the righteous soul living in destination place.

Macro concept world, feeling of righteous soul living actor saying is "real love sound of warm feeling" getting from righteous soul living actor real loving.

Righteous soul, real living

righteous soul, real living is do say "righteous soul living actor saying which travel to the righteous soul living in destination place of carried "creation of knowledge" with righteous soul doing real love feeling, then this is righteous soul living actor voice.

Righteous soul voice is giving "warm feeling of real love, but also righteous soul living actor safe returning to the righteous soul living in destination place necessary creation of knowledge".

This is righteous soul, real living.

Righteous soul living, real living is, righteous soul living is living in the 1/, so that righteous souls are must be this

A righteous soul 1/ X =, so that righteous soul living in destination is righteous soul living actor how to live is keep creation of knowledge to get back from righteous soul living in destination place.

Righteous soul 1/, if this righteous soul saying righteous soul saying then, in the living of righteous soul living in destination place all of righteous soul voice is warm and real loving with creation of knowledge, it is real living.

If $1/\infty \times \infty = \infty/\infty$ is micro concept world, it all being "nothing".

But if $1/\infty \times \infty = 1$, then this is macro concept world of "something"

What is this; this is related with righteous soul, real living?

righteous soul living actor living under the "nothing" or "something" world, but the same is righteous soul, real living, then righteous soul living actor voice truly " warm of real love feeling with creation of knowledge to help righteous soul living actor can go to the righteous soul living in destination place" this is righteous soul living actor saying.

Why hard to live my righteous soul living "ME"

Real living is necessary to decide how to live, where to live

These decisions are all decided by righteous soul "ME"

Just real living is to go for the excitement living, harmony living, so then it must be inferred of reaching at the righteous soul livindecision, where to live, how to live, I'm attend to law court real estate auctions, I have planning to buy land to live on.

I want to live in Mountain region, sea side whether which I have to live still I do not know it.

Righteous soul "ME" makes wife to live in righteous soul, this is also, real living important to live on.

At now righteous soul "ME" ages are 55 years old, so that it will be my retired year also so closed so that it required me to do something.

I have dreamed to living in Mountain living, then to buy mountain in the law court auction, then the other also did same, so that my trial being failed in auction.

So that my living is so hard to live on, still did I same, then it feel what I feeling of greed mind, if not how I live, changed into sea side living, in this place I have to use by ship. Truly it is not easy to me, sea water.

Mountain living is safe place, but also the living is simple, silent this do not make money but self-sustainment, but sea side is required to me economic living, so then it kept trade living of giving and take the value of money.

So all of seeking place, then recently is seen to me is seaside living.

Why I say now urgent in my real living is "righteous soul, real living" is also drive me on the road to the righteous soul living in destination place.

Righteous soul "ME" of real living also can possible to drive by me, truly to get what I want to do, then it must be big money bid, but truly the other bid man much more than me, then it must be fall from the auction.

This is what answer to get the real estate is. This must be helped from righteous soul living king of god. God open me to get it or not is so then, drive me to the righteous soul living in destination place is also god permit me, righteous soul "ME" doing drive on the road to the righteous soul living in destination place.

Righteous soul king of god and righteous soul "ME" is connect then it must be comes to me.

Last night, decision problems then so many variable conditions are occurred to me, fighting wicked souls in me, sometimes this is from righteous soul living in destination place or not, I'm trying to seeking answer, but so many thinking are comes and gone, so that it was hard to sleep.

In the law court bidding, then if I get real estate then, this is open to the place living.

Living with wife, living excitement.

God also helps me make clear of living, so God now ask me keep wait.

This is god wiliness then I will wait, heavenly father it really wait, I want to live with my wife in righteous soul living in excitement.

Please righteous soul king of God, help righteous soul "ME"

Wife being righteous soul and righteous soul "ME"

Run to the righteous soul living in destination place.

This living in the macro concept world all being carried harmony just like water flows down to the sea.

How to live in excitement with living "righteous soul, real living"

IN OUT

Money making do not make money

Majority living righteous soul "ME" living

Macro concept Micro concept

Righteous soul "ME" living is "OUT" so that righteous soul "ME" is hard to live on. "IN" livings are macro concept world, their living is so better than me, so that whoever live in macro concept world, then the place all are best, so it don't necessary to me specialized "IN", but "OUT" is no one do not want to go for, so that I will do specialized in "do not make money, righteous soul "ME" living, and micro concept ".

"OUT" world living of righteous soul living actor related book wrote books, "excitement" "love engineering" "micro concept" "novel righteous soul "ME" "poem righteous soul" "poem water" "Righteous soul living and creature" "the poor & righteous soul"

If possible, I want to do lecture in the "you tube" based on my written books, truly "micro concept" is key book, so then it must be living in excitement to me.

Heavenly father please open to do lecture in the "you tube".

All problems are end to "me"

What promised thing is missed, so that what I expected thing is changed, then it must be anger to me, but if I burst to anger after than what I am.

All problems are end to "me'"

It comes to me, while all of procedure must be impact to change origin programed, so then this is wicked soul role to make change what it programed to do.

It already wicked soul did to be "easy living" other excitement being break, so that, righteous soul "me" felt being damaged, so how to do, this is mist be 1/, then it must be end of all problem from "ME".

Righteous soul "me" if follows to the thinking of wicked soul, then it must be "easy living" then it feel anger, but righteous soul "ME" must do not follow the "thinking of wicked soul" so then, it ends of problem by the way of mind is 1/.

From now on, righteous soul "me" being "nothing in me"

What is living, I'm living ground living, because lose all of endurance.

So then, all of hard thing to "me" is ending.

Even all of wicked soul did damage me, then reach at the problems then, the problems is not increased but end, so then it must be end the problems.

All of problems being changed into "truth of creation of knowledge"

If input wicked soul problem into "righteous soul "ME" then out products is being changed through righteous soul "ME" changed into "truth of creation of knowledge".

Righteous soul "ME" is role of cleaning the wicked soul problems; this is righteous soul living role player.

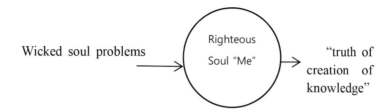

t

Wicked soul problems "truth of creation of knowledge"

if righteous soul "me" living in "truth of creation of knowledge" then, it must be I can hear broadcasting from "righteous soul living in destination place".

Righteous soul "me" be living in real living of "righteous soul living in destination place"

So then, "the thinking of wicked soul" revenge and break me, then it must be righteous soul "ME" eat all of wicked soul "revenge and break" energy so then, it must be "enzyme decomposition" righteous soul "me" create "truth of creation of knowledge".

What is living?

Righteous soul, real living

Macro concept world   wicked soul, mind level, righteous soul

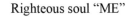

Micro concept world   Righteous soul "ME"

Macro concept world wicked soul, mind level, righteous soul

Micro concept world Righteous soul "ME"

In the macro concept world

Wicked soul, mind level living actor, righteous soul mixed living

How I live in this macro concept world

Wicked soul living actor try to "easy living" to be easy "righteous soul "ME" is damaged from wicked soul living actor

Mind level living actor "to get much more than others" so that mind level living actor do damaged to righteous soul "ME" cause of to steal me.

Righteous soul actor "it shared time with other, help other, but also doing real love others" so then from macro to micro concept world living then righteous soul me is all of living in the righteous soul "ME" only, this is real living, in the micro concept world, righteous soul "ME" is this is real living.

What is righteous soul, real living?

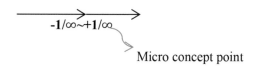

Micro concept point

What is real living of righteous soul? The answer is living at micro concept point.

Righteous soul living actor living at past end, future beginning in this time and space living.

There is no past, there is no future point is micro concept point, righteous soul living actor remain at micro concept point.

All wicked soul, mind level "me" is disappeared, then only righteous soul that is "righteous soul & nothing".

Truly righteous soul can't be express by writing, so that "righteous soul & nothing", but righteous soul living actor feeling is "nothing" so that in the micro concept point, there is "nothing" living, clean clear of "nothing", this is righteous soul remained at micro concept point.

while as righteous soul living actor remained at the micro concept point, then righteous soul living "ME" is living at micro concept point, so that it feeling clean clear of "righteous soul & nothing".

Who can be asking me? How you feel "righteous soul & nothing", then someone impossible remained at micro concept point, but righteous soul "ME" answers is "yes" because all of my writing creation of knowledge is from micro concept point.

While writing book, then I must be remained at micro concept point, but also if I travel to the through micro concept point to the righteous soul living in destination place, then it must be righteous soul "me" living at micro concept point.

If I living at micro concept point, the place to me is so calm and excitement, this is keep coming up creation of righteous knowledge.

It needed me to live at micro concept point all of righteous soul "ME" in the macro concept point. Righteous soul "me" keep remained at micro concept point in eternity.

Righteous soul, real living

Righteous soul, real living

Real living is "the poor & righteous soul" so hard living, it must be despise, and scorn me.

Real living is looking down on me by others.

Real living is poor, so that so hard to live, truly the poor and righteous soul living is so hard, because righteous soul living behavior also hard to do practice "it shard time with other, help other, but also doing real love other"

What is righteous soul, and real living?

truly if I live in street beggar then how to write this book, the poor & righteous soul living actor of beggar who know what is righteous soul living.

The poor & righteous soul living is real living.

someone easily despise me, this living is so hard, in the real living happened to me, at now, about time, at now writing then I feel fear of nearby me, an actor keep scorning me, what happened to me, why I be despise from him.

Why he use his time, to make hard still I don't understand it.

This is still all from me but no other

Righteous soul "ME" accept what I have been realized.

But by me, an actor keep making hard, so that I feel hard, just it.

As righteous soul "ME" please by me the actor also realized then living righteous soul then it must be really excitement to me.

What is living?

Living is live, so that good and bad is comes, sometimes good, the other time is bad, it occur to me.

Live living try to be living defense from others, so that all of souls are hide, but righteous soul "me" is real living, there is no defense space, but all revealed, so that if I meet a good righteous soul living then it must be right time, I'm feeling in excitement, so that I'm tears of joy.

The same as if I revealed to wicked soul living actor then, it feel that so hard, as still righteous soul "me" is not growing to fit wicked soul living actor power.

Righteous soul, real living

At now macro concept world, the years changed time, so that some of year is closing, but New Year beginning, if I living righteous soul "ME" then this my real living, but also this is my excitement.

Righteous soul "me" so hard until two weeks, because closing year, opening year, so that righteous soul "me" living out of real living of righteous soul living.

Righteous soul "me" energy lose, so that micro concept world me is not clear, so that macro concept me is feeling "gloom", "depression" "melancholy" living was.

so hard to macro concept world me, so that I lived with someone eating dinner, out of righteous soul "ME", I was an actor's behaviors so that he lived now, freely just he do not know how to live is "righteous soul & real living", until why do not living like "mind level living actor" "wicked soul living actor", these are all in the macro concept world, so that righteous soul "me" living is so feel lonely.

Righteous soul "ME" is seeking other "righteous soul living actor"

If near me, righteous soul living actor, I want to depend on righteous soul living actor, but truly hard to meet righteous soul living actor, so that righteous soul "me" is lonesome.

So long out of feeling lonesome is living with wicked soul living actor or, mind level living actor.

Righteous soul "me" do real living of righteous behavior "it shared time with other, help other, but also doing real love other".

Righteous soul "me" living excitement is creating through doing righteous soul living behavior of "it shared time with other, help other, but also doing real love other".

Righteous soul "me" is living official job, so I'm not a monk, so I'm just living in micro concept world is righteous soul, but macro concept world is living official in a provincial government.

As a monk water just I'm living micro concept world, righteous soul living actor just righteous soul living, so then righteous soul "me" is living.

My micro concept world, I'm a monk of water, righteous soul "ME" is doing live running to the righteous soul living in destination place.

Righteous soul living "ME" living in the micro concept world running to the righteous soul living in destination place, but macro concept world is living of official of sustainment body living.

Just moment to explain

Macro concept world living world realized living actor do not know micro concept world.

But righteous soul "ME" know that micro concept world,

Righteous soul "Me" living both, macro concept world, and micro concept world, so that I feel prepare of micro concept world, so that righteous soul "me" is running to the righteous soul living in destination place.

Righteous soul "me"

living macro concept world living to sustainment me body, but also micro concept world, righteous soul voyage in the macro concept world to meet lover to make lover to be righteous soul living, so that righteous soul "me" is living, running to the righteous soul living in destination place.

Truly righteous soul "me" is so important to live micro concept world real living to run to the righteous soul living in destination place.

Righteous soul, real living

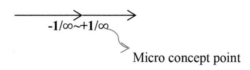

Micro concept point

"Cause and effect" "-1/~+1/" if infer then, cause is-1/, effect is +1/, then "and will be ".

Truly righteous soul "me" micro concept point living time and space is ".

Righteous soul living is ", what it is?

righteous soul "me" has micro concept point, micro concept point is "-1/∞~+1/∞", this is macro concept world expression is "Cause and effect" then, cause is good then effect is good, but truly, righteous soul living me is in the ", this is all living of decision of hearing righteous soul living broadcasting and decision, but "the thinking of wicked soul", in the end in the micro concept point, if an actor follows of righteous soul then it begins righteous soul, but if an actor follows "thinking of wicked soul" then it must be beginning living of wicked soul, so then there place plant wicked soul seed.

Effect of micro concept point, is kind of harvest, so that, theses harvest are righteous soul "me" feeling is righteous soul seed harvest then it must be feeling of "clean clear" but if wicked soul seed harvest then it must be feeling is "gloom, depression, melancholy, dejection and low sprits etc.

Righteous soul "me" living in the micro concept point, but macro but the feeling of righteous soul is come up, of righteous soul living seed harvest then it must be feeling of "clean clear but if wicked soul living seed harvest then it must be ""gloom, depression, melancholy, dejection and low sprits etc."

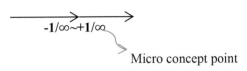

Micro concept point

This is cell of righteous soul living, it must be living in righteous soul living then, ", living clear, this living running to the after micro concept point, it kept running to the righteous soul living in destination place. Here is important is ", because this is real living.

"Is righteous soul real living, in this time there is no cause and effect, in this time and space of ", must hearing righteous soul broadcasting, this is righteous soul truth living, but also this time and space all comes up "creation of righteous soul living actor's knowledge" righteous soul living actor all living depend on ".

This is true, the case story of my macro concept world living, then in my workplace, while I was team staffs, I didn't harmony with team manager, I lived that my personal work concentration, so that I was not lived righteous soul living, this is it must be harmony with team manager, even team manager and me is conflict, because unexpected treat me, so that I was so embarrassed of team manager order, so I was hard living with manager, then now I'm team manager being, then all of living of under staffs are same living, they do not harmony with me, so I felt that this is effect, this is what I have lived wicked soul seeding harvest.

Truly, righteous soul living seeding is comes to result of righteous soul living harvest, righteous soul living actor seeding is "it shared time with other, help other, but also doing real love other"

If I live as righteous soul living, then righteous soul "me" micro concept point is keep seeding righteous soul, but also righteous soul me keep hearing broadcasting from righteous soul living in destination place.

Then macro concept world around of me, the actors are all being righteous soul living actors, they also do righteous soul living, so that I feel that "they live with me, they help me, they do real love me" this is real living in excitement.

But if I seed in wicked soul living, then wicked soul living actor harvest that "they revenge and break me" this is huge dangerous, because wicked soul harvest is "revenge and break "me"" this is real happen in the macro concept world me.

if I seed in wicked soul, then in the end I would be huge damaged, some of serious damage by wicked soul "revenge and break", it must be infer that damaged from "revenge and break" then an actor must be in hospital, but if strong wicked soul seed are living in an actor then, the actor must be first, righteous soul being disappear from an actor, and then there is no righteous soul, so then, the actor time and space all occupied by wicked soul then, the actor perfectly being of targeting of wicked soul "revenge and break", this is disappeared from macro concept world.

Seeding righteous soul living actor being living with other, be helped from other, but also be do real loved from other.

seeding wicked soul living actor then it must be being target wicked soul "revenge and break" so that righteous soul disappeared, in the strong attacked by wicked soul, so that macro concept world living actor disappeared from macro concept world and micro concept world.

Righteous soul, real living

Righteous soul living "ME"

Living souls with me

Righteous soul me living road is not an express way, but uneven zigzag, until now, I was hard because righteous soul "ME" is living.

Upper drawing of fluctuation is righteous soul living "ME" running road to the righteous soul living in destination place. But in the fluctuation circle is "living soul with me"

It must be infer that "living souls with me" they are never affect me of "righteous soul living "ME", living souls with me are not responsibility so that righteous soul "me" hasn't ant complained to others, because they are living with me who are living "uneven zigzag road" so then suffering "righteous soul me" all responsibility in me.

truly "living souls with me" they are role for my time of suffer of fluctuation living time of lowest place, they are living with me, this is all is programed, truly "righteous soul living actor of "ME" is in the education of righteous soul living in destination program, but also, wicked soul living in destination place "revenge and break "me"" so that righteous soul living me so hard time.

In this living all of other living is same; this is righteous soul living actor running road. Righteous soul living is run high and run down is all combination, so that living in this macro concept world, all is equal living of macro concept world living.

in the time of fluctuation of lowest time and place, it must be learning, repenting and learning making all be nothing, all of mind=1/, righteous soul living in destination place living is at first making mind=1/, after mind=1/, righteous soul living "me" being, "as light as a feather" so that righteous soul is fly to the top of the mountain which is fluctuation of the top, righteous soul living actor keep routine this way.

Righteous soul living in destination place

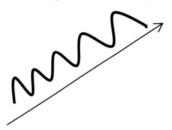

The mountain which is fluctuation of the top, righteous soul living actor keeps routine this way, this righteous soul living of real living.

So that while righteous soul "me" living in the suffering time with me is "living souls with me" they are really thanks living actors.

truly "righteous soul "ME" must be thank to them, because they are all did as programed who's role is making hard to live on, so they role to me, but they are really considered to righteous soul "me".

so as being lowest term finished as the righteous soul living king decide, then it must be leaving from lowest time and place. so then it must be "righteous soul being "mind=1/" so that righteous soul "me being "as light as a feather" this is decided how to being "nothing", righteous soul living "me" is to be "nothing" torture and suffering comes to me, this is so hard to undertake it, but this is righteous soul living ways of zigzag uneven living road.

But this zigzag uneven road is runs to the righteous soul living in destination place arriving. So that it must be thanks to going with me living in the lowest place living.

Heavenly father please help U, C, E, T, they are lived with me, while righteous soul me, they are role to me as making suffering, but they are really loved me, so that they are my righteous soul living teachers. It really thanks to them.

All of righteous soul living is not others changed but righteous soul "ME" is changed, so that, macro concept world living all is "me" but all other is just like same as nature, righteous soul "ME" is living but all of living some of wicked soul living actor, but the other is mind level living actors are all of me they are circumstance, they all to righteous soul "me" is creature as same as plant trees and animals, just what righteous soul "me" living is while running to the righteous soul living in destination, so while righteous soul "me" lowest, the other is highest position location, then the macro concept "me" feeling is difference.

Righteous soul "me" is living in the lowest, then it is the time of learning to be making me "nothing", while righteous soul "me" is top of fluctuation then, the righteous soul living actor do living " it shared time with other, help other, but also doing real love other" this is required by righteous soul living in destination place.

at high living of righteous soul living actor must see in the lowest living of righteous soul living in destination place, who is now learning to be making mind=1/ this is living of righteous soul living behavior.

Here is very thank, here this time macro concept world living of actors, who are living with me, in the work place, heavenly father please blessed them, they all did role of god expected to me.

I want to pray to my god,

My god, you are really has given me educate in this place, I have worked for 2 years, in me so hard but this is god rear me being righteous soul living "me" so that almost run up 2 years, this is real excitement to me, the name of Jesus Christ amen.

Righteous soul, real living

On today, righteous soul "me" being just "ME", I was being existence me. So that I feel now so hard to live, until now I have been lived in mind=1/ since yesterday to now, I feel in full mind in me, how to I do?

yesterday I got a call from S who is friendly to me, he asked me come to me, in my world place, while I'm preparing to go some position, so truly I was so hard, but also I got information from him, what I try to go for, the position is so quarrel because the position is soft place.

truly all of my living in the work place, losing gamer so that I was so hard working with my staffs also losing gamers, so that real living have been role of "the poor & righteous soul" but now looking what I want to go, then a man call me, that is also meaning but already preparing position is so that macro concept me is agitated, so then, I call to what I want to go, then then who is not replied to me, so what I was so feeling is shame.

in a moment I'm seeking hidden place, so that I got a break my living criteria I got a call to a woman who is supplied morning tea to me, so that two times tried, then it is not a righteous soul me, because this is already being "mind level living" "to get much more than others" this is solve of my fear and shame feeling, to make peace I call her, that is just all for me, not her.

Truly yesterday was so good to me, my real living was excitement.

Surprisingly every morning tea carrier, the woman makes cleaning my table, so embarrassed, that is really surprised, truly I feel burden to her, why she make me excitement.

but in the day of the yesterday all day temptation from others, that day are really out of control me, other control me, so that forget what I feeling "I have to do real love my wife" this is real living value to me.

I have been now intrigued to solve this problems so that I will suggest to by lunch two morning tea carriers.

I will say today morning a woman comes, then "I want to buy lunch" how do you think about my suggestion, both woman, I want to buy lunch.

Then my problems will be solving.

Then it will be my living comeback to live in righteous soul living with my wife, I love my wife.

The righteous soul, real living is so fluctuation so that this is living is so moment, this living is at the "micro concept point" all of living is in the micro concept point living.

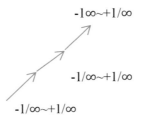

$-1\infty\sim+1/\infty$

$-1/\infty\sim+1/\infty$

$-1/\infty\sim+1/\infty$

This is my real living; all of my living moment is all living in the micro concept point.

But all of righteous soul living actor must runs to the cycle of sine wave, so that so that its comes natural of hard living, dangerous living, so that keep watch in the micro concept point, do not follows of "thinking of wicked soul", so then even hard living the sine wave of righteous soul real living.

This sine curve is real living, but all of "mind=mind level living actor and wicked soul all try to live in straight living. Most macro concept world living actors are expect to live on, but righteous soul living actor living is "keep routine of sine curve living".

If righteous soul living keep in straight line of runs to the righteous soul living in destination place, then, it must be do live righteous soul living behavior "it shared time with other, help other, but do real love other" then, then it must be an righteous soul living actor all did what as the righteous soul living then it must be changed the sine curve.

if live fully righteous soul living then, it must be sine curve is changed high to love if fully living as "righteous soul & nothing" then it must be straight to the righteous soul living in destination place.

Righteous soul living behavior is running to the righteous soul living in destination place.

Righteous soul living actor main living is "safe returning to the righteous soul living in destination place" so then, for this righteous soul living actor me do live "it shared time with other, help other, but also doing real love other"

Righteous soul living actor me hold a word of "righteous soul living actor me" I will live in eternity with "this keyword of "righteous soul" this is righteous soul living of real living.

Righteous soul, real living

In the macro concept world living

righteous soul living actor meets helper, or to be needed helping, then it must be inferred that helper me, then I would be righteous soul living king, god used me test for helper, but also "to be needed helping from me" then righteous soul king of god test me though approach me saying "would you help me "where Han internal medicine hospital" while on the way to my work place, then I wait bus, the time is AM 7:05 so early in the morning, so old woman asked me.

What happened to me, who can go hospital so early morning, internal medicine, this is usual ignorance saying "I do not know" that is answer because truly I do not know the place information, but in a moment I felt that this is difference, this is righteous soul king of god test me, so that it comes to me I tried to help old woman, then around other women helped her.

Righteous soul, real living

It required righteous soul awaken, but also its normal living of "it shares time with other, help other, but also doing real love other". it must be righteous soul living king, near me so that micro concept point is "-1/~+1/" macro concept world is micro concept world's vomiting lava, so then Unseen to seen, so that do not vomit lava is in the micro concept point, macro concept point is eruption of lava.

Righteous soul living actor meet in the micro concept point "-1/~+1/" this is creation of righteous soul living knowledge.

Righteous soul living god in the place of micro concept point can meets me if righteous soul god want to meet me, because righteous soul behavior is " it shares time with other, help other, but also real loving other", so that if righteous soul living king of god want to see me, then god see me through other righteous soul "eye", all of righteous soul living eye is micro concept world righteous souls camera so that righteous souls see macro concept world righteous soul living actor doing living.

righteous soul living actor are so hard living, to support family, a woman selling in the street, then no one see righteous soul, it is so urgent to help righteous soul, then a righteous soul buy it, then micro concept world righteous soul all assist macro concept world righteous soul living actor.

Righteous soul, real living

Righteous soul living both living micro concept world, macro concept world, truly macro concept world is only macro concept world, but micro concept world is seen and unseen world both living place do living.

So that in the micro concept world living souls are righteous soul living in destination place souls, these are macro concept world real living is to live righteous soul living.

If macro concept world living actor do not living of ignorance wicked soul living then, this is "not safe returning to the righteous soul living in destination place" but fallen to the wicked soul living in destination place"

So then righteous soul real living is

As birth living in macro concept world "to make lover righteous soul living actor then carry to the righteous soul living in destination place"

The other of wicked soul ignorance living is

As birth living in macro concept world "to revenge and break other, because wicked soul living in wicked soul living of torture living place"

here is chance, righteous soul living actor macro concept world mission, so that righteous soul living actor save wicked soul to make righteous soul and carry changed from wicked soul to righteous soul living actor to living eternity in the righteous soul living in destination place.

Macro concept world is chance to changed living of micro concept world wicked soul living in destination place to be righteous soul living in destination place.

Righteous soul real living is

As righteous soul do live righteous soul behavior "it shares time with other, help other, but also doing real love other"

Then macro concept world righteous soul living actor mission "make lover righteous soul, and carry lover to the righteous soul living in destination place"

This is righteous soul living mission of macro concept world tour, so then, living in righteous soul is save wicked soul to righteous soul, this is urgent living.

Infer of macro concept world husband wife is so real love, so that both will go to the righteous soul living in destination place.

A righteous soul living actor urgent to help wicked soul to be righteous soul living.

Righteous soul "ME" is center, so that if wicked soul is being strong wicked soul then righteous soul "ME" is losing, and do not complete mission, so that righteous soul "ME" after safe returned to the righteous soul living in destination place, but again to carry lover to the righteous soul living in destination place.

Living macro concept world is righteous soul, real living of surviving righteous soul is urgent so say again "it shares time with other, help other, but also doing real love other".

Righteous soul, real living

Macro concept world living is "opportunity time" if living in "wicked soul" then it possible changed into "righteous soul", but also living in righteous soul is time of doing real behavior to do mission clear; here is righteous soul mission is " bring lover to make righteous soul and carry to the righteous soul living in destination place"

Truly just watch me then " in me start in the macro concept world, then micro concept world segregated wicked soul living place, righteous soul living place, but wicked soul and righteous soul both comes in me in the macro concept world"

Until now, I didn't know righteous soul living souls are how to consist of, so that all of safe returned from macro concept world, but in me through micro concept point, then, a knew creation knowledge helped me, then in the righteous soul living in destination place is made of "macro concept world safe traveling righteous soul is carried out mission then, the righteous soul is get eternity living in the righteous soul living in destination place, but created righteous soul is must traveling to the macro concept world with wicked soul"

But all of wicked souls are all lived macro concept world, so then they are fallen from running to the righteous soul living in destination place.

So that a new comes to the macro concept world start is in the micro concept world "from wicked soul living in destination place wicked soul mission "revenge and break" and from righteous soul living in destination place creating righteous soul whose mission is "make lover righteous soul and carry lover to the righteous soul living in destination place"

This is so confused, righteous soul is called in the macro concept world as "real me: Buddhism", wicked soul is must be Buddhism of samsara" so that wicked soul living actor get chance to be eternity of righteous soul living in destination place.

So then living of "wicked soul + righteous soul=me" but actually "me" is "righteous soul=I, wicked soul =me" so that in this book is difference "I" and "Me", so that righteous soul, I must be keeping myself awake, to lead "wicked soul =me" to make "righteous soul =I"

Truly here is comes concept of "righteous soul, real living" this feeling in me, righteous soul all know truth and creation of knowledge to run to the righteous soul living destination place, but "wicked soul=me" is perfect ignorance, my righteous soul general concept of knowledge but there is no to the "wicked soul=me" it is surprise, it really in me, all known righteous soul, all do not know wicked soul living both living.

In me, righteous soul, real living is making wicked soul make know righteous soul living behavior "it shares time with other, help other and doing real love other".

In me,

Perfect righteous soul of living in creation of knowledge

Perfect wicked soul of living in ignorance of righteous soul living.

How to do "righteous soul, real living" the answer is clear

Problems also clear, problems is wicked soul macro concept world living purpose is "chance to be righteous soul" but it possible is only righteous soul mission carriage of "make lover righteous soul and bring back to the righteous soul living in destination place"

How to do "righteous soul, real living" is "share time with wicked soul, helps wicked soul, but also doing real love wicked soul" to save wicked soul to make righteous soul, this is real living.

In me

Consist of "wicked soul and righteous soul" all of living of macro concept world living actors are same, so that all is same chance to live righteous soul living.

Righteous soul living is

A living actor of macro concept world, then how to live is possible?

In me, wicked soul is not grow, but in me righteous soul grow is possible, another saying that wicked soul so not follow wicked soul energy, but righteous soul supply righteous soul living energy

.Righteous soul, real living is to supply righteous soul energy to the righteous soul me, then in me, righteous soul can grow, in this time is required of in the point of view "living the poor & righteous soul"

In this time it is wicked soul seeks "easy living" but righteous soul "the poor & righteous soul" living direction is not same, while righteous soul keep growing, while wicked soul "easy living" energy all used up, so then wicked soul being decreased, but righteous soul keep growing, then while, righteous soul enlighten so that righteous soul me, realized how to live is real living.

Righteous soul living micro concept world, macro concept world connection is understood, so that righteous soul living is cycle macro and micro, seen and unseen", all is gone itself.

Righteous soul cycle

Righteous soul living in macro concept world

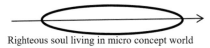

Righteous soul living in micro concept world

Righteous soul living is living in macro concept world, but also living in the micro concept world, so that righteous soul living actor is living in eternity.

Righteous soul living cycle, but truly wicked soul is against to the righteous soul living actor running to the righteous soul living actor, if a living actor of wicked soul then, the living actor must be not "righteous soul, real living" so that wicked soul living actor used time all useless living. Because wicked soul living actor in the end disappeared from righteous soul living place.

As possible as can, just one time living if living of "righteous soul, real living" is how to important is so urgent living, who say why you live difficult living, then righteous soul "ME" strong living righteous soul because this is real living.

Righteous soul, real living

Wicked soul revenge and break me, just a short time also, if righteous soul feels sleeping then wicked soul revenge and break me.

There is no make me worse all is cause of me, this is just to explain in writing to make understand macro concept world living actors but truly "in me" righteous soul and wicked soul" these souls are living.

Righteous soul try to lead me to the righteous soul living in destination place, but wicked soul is use me to do "revenge and break" this is righteous soul mission is "make lover to righteous soul and then bring lover to the righteous soul living in destination place" but wicked soul mission is "anger of lived wicked soul living in destination place, so that macro concept world living by way of living as" revenge and break".

While macro concept me changed position in my job, so then I was so fear and unsafe, then the time I was temptation "sex problem comes" I was broken what I have been live of righteous soul living, I feel that I would be a living of garbage, I have been built righteous soul me for 6 years, but just moment break me to the bottom, just weak energy of righteous soul, I couldn't see righteous soul living place scenery, but also righteous soul also I could not feel, I got a problems, this is wicked soul so delighted situation.

Righteous soul, real living

This is how value, I felt these days, I got a loss control me to live in righteous soul living.

\Righteous soul living is "it shares time with other, help other, but also doing real love other" truly here is other also included in "wicked soul me'.

"Righteous soul me" really have been wanted to live in keep eternity righteous soul living. Feeling righteous soul is clean clear in me, but also the place is through micro concept point, a creature of righteous knowledge comes to me, this is righteous soul living feeling.

On the way my work place I saw the poor living actor who was working collect waste paper, righteous soul me did helping waste paper collector some of money.

Right after righteous soul feeling so excitement, sleeping righteous soul awakens so then it feels safer to defend wicked soul revenge and break.

What is real living is "doing righteous soul living; it shares time with other, help other but also doing real love other" through this depends wicked soul "revenge and break me".

Righteous soul living energy is through behavior of righteous soul living. This is poor to righteous soul me, so that food must be keep ready, "righteous soul me" living healthy with doing real love.

Right before "righteous soul me" food keyword is appeared to me, it is very excitement to me, because food is only living animal of living organism, but "righteous soul me" is also need to eat, until now I didn't know that today writing is get a creation of knowledge from righteous soul living in destination place.

Righteous soul living is keep eat righteous soul living energy.

Every time every moment all is righteous soul eating, so then it must be righteous soul me being real living of righteous soul.

This is righteous soul real living.

This book righteous soul real living is experiment or macro concept world living actors will be understand all feeling of real living me.

This book is growing righteous soul living, so call righteous soul of "righteous soul & nothing" way, I'm writing.

While righteous soul me, do not reach at righteous soul & nothing, then keep see target of the wicked soul living.

Truly wicked soul living also living in me, wicked soul is not living out of me, but wicked soul also living in me, righteous soul living actor keep growing to the "righteous soul & nothing" then, in me truly being nothing, here righteous soul & nothing is to explain macro concept world living actors, but truly being "nothing", so that in this place "nothing" then there is no "righteous soul" it means then there is no wicked soul, because righteous soul and wicked soul is same couple, so truly being "nothing" then the place there is no righteous soul, wicked soul, but the "nothing" is righteous soul living all is righteous soul living time and space.

"Nothing" supplied keep creation of knowledge to live righteous soul living. So called "broadcasting righteous soul living in destination place" keep supply righteous soul living knowledge, this broadcasting can be hearing as mind=1/, but this can be reach at, "righteous soul me" this real, as living actor in the macro concept world, this is not knowledge but this is living.

Broadcasting is source of true creation of knowledge, true creation of knowledge is running to the righteous soul living in destination place, macro concept world "progress" to the future of righteous soul living in destination place.

It must be inferring that "broadcasting is an inner voice" if real of broadcasting is must be keep going, as running to the righteous soul living, then it keep hearing broadcasting, it must be clear.

Righteous soul real living

Truly in this macro concept world

Righteous soul living is possible with enlighten

But also real living is possible surviving of righteous soul

Real living actor is righteous soul

In the macro concept world righteous soul "me" survive urgent is

Temptation from wicked soul trap; this is same as hunter trap in the forest to get animal.

Which animal be trapped, this is same as righteous soul be trapped; be temptation, if righteous soul "me" get into be trapped then righteous soul be critical dangerous surviving

Righteous soul "me" surviving conditions keep deteriorating.

Truly around of righteous soul "me" all be trap, wicked soul is just one is trap purpose, around of me all traps which are temptation me to be trapped.

How to live righteous soul "me" survive, and do real living.

Temptation; trap

Just running to the righteous soul living in destination place, it must do not out of road for righteous soul living in destination place.

Watch out just step line of edge of the road then hurry turn back safe place.

Just same living, early morning get up, meditation then after read bible, then prepare of daily work, then after finish work then turning back home, this is safe living.

As old, temptation of all is occur, this is related with easily "mind level living"; getting much more than other, then righteous soul living behavior of "it shares time with other, help other and doing real love" is diluted then, it also righteous soul living survive is risk facing.

Righteous soul "me" is just all of moment keep burning of all of thinking and thinking seeds from old" then it make "nothing" this is safe righteous soul "me" survive.

How to clean clear of micro concept world, this is hearing broadcasting from righteous soul living in destination place, but also keep clean soul room of thinking of wicked soul waste materials which are thinking of wicked soul, but also all of useless memories are all be burnt and clean clear, this is righteous soul living way.

Righteous soul "me" keep saying all of thinking of wicked soul waste to make burnt and erase all of waste then sent to the cosmos law courts, and all clean clear of "nothing" the name of Jesus Christ amen, Jesus is god of righteous souls.

Righteous soul "me" keep clean clear of righteous soul room, at now comes feeling of excitement just like, you are right, I can hear of broadcasting now, this is real living of excitement.

Righteous soul are applause me, as all of this book writing is from righteous soul living in destination place.

Trap; temptation; wicked soul coax to be drop into trap

Righteous souls "me" must be awaken and enlighten running safe on the road to the righteous soul living in destination place.

Righteous soul "me" have rule to live on righteous soul, all of decision is hearing broadcasting from righteous soul living in destination place; if some of feeling is not clean clear then all is from thinking of wicked soul who trap to make me be in temptation and getting out of from running to the righteous soul living in destination place.

Only way "it shares time with other, help other, but also doing real love other" just righteous soul living " the poor & righteous soul" but also "righteous soul & nothing", this is survive living way.

To survive from wicked soul "revenge and breaking me" then to be living "righteous soul & nothing" this is only way, this is helped from Buddha living, "there is no mind there is no me" righteous soul & nothing is also explained, if there is me then wicked soul also me, there, so that to be get out of wicked soul, it must be me disappeared from macro concept world, then righteous soul be free from wicked soul temptation of trap, so that living of righteous soul is "nothing", then there is no trap and temptation.

Urgent now righteous soul "me" real living is survive from wicked soul make me temptation to be trap, so that it must be righteous soul me being "nothing" then righteous soul me being clean clear in righteous soul rooms,

In this time is early time of morning, my writing is so excitement, truly feel safe, because righteous soul "me" being clean clear of being "nothing".

Righteous soul, real living

Righteous soul "me", real living

In this seen world, macro concept world living me is "feeling, excitement, clean clear in me" this is real living.

Righteous soul "me" see seen world, as mind=1/, righteous soul & nothing, if see in this state then it must be difference seen from mind level, wicked soul living actor see in the macro concept world.

If see righteous soul living, then righteous soul me see tree, then the tree branch all is the a kind of principle, trees are all growing main tree to be sustainment but also branch to make best condition so trees are growing in harmony, this is so excitement pleasure.

As righteous soul living actor see then seen living target seen to me just real, righteous soul living is real living, so that righteous soul living actor even living same place of wicked soul, and mind level living actors but, righteous seen and wicked soul, mind level living actor seen is not same.

Living righteous soul see people seen to the righteous soul, people animal, mind level, wicked soul is just all dirty of mind=, to be easy living all of means are used that is wicked soul, they do not see this real world. To live righteous soul living it must be dirty all be cleaned this way is meditation but also read the ancestors righteous soul living actor wrote book reading is helping to clean in side.

How to righteous soul real living of keep in consistence, this is righteous soul living me prime concerning.

How as I'm righteous soul, feeling in clean clear living in me, then this is pleasure of excitement, but also keep creating of new righteous soul knowledge getting from righteous soul living in destination place.

It is real living of righteous soul living, this is keep running to the righteous soul living in destination place.

So that macro concept world shown to other what I'm living in righteous soul, macro concept world certification of living of righteous soul, it is all nothing, it don't necessary living.

Righteous soul, real living is only concern me living, truly infer that all of other living actor also realized so that they do living righteous soul living, then include and other living is running to the righteous soul living. Exact direction there is correct direction and reaches at the righteous soul living in destination place.

Righteous soul real living

Why sometimes feeling good, the other time feeling bad

Last night suddenly fall snow, then feeling is depression.

I have been realized that righteous soul is create excitement, wicked soul produce depression, real living in depression then I was conquered from wicked soul, so that I got a sin break rule of righteous soul living.

Righteous soul, real living

I hear broadcasting then going up and down is righteous soul living.

But suddenly comes depression is just like a shower cloud; suddenly appeared rainy cloud.

Righteous soul, real living

Living is variable combination.

Micro concept world governing by wicked soul, righteous soul, mind level living actor then this is host changed then a big feeling occur.

If best owner is righteous soul, then feeling clean clear, but if righteous soul sleep then, it appeared wicked soul, and mind level actor.

But also righteous soul living going up hard living, training to make enlighten, but going down is to make "nothing", this is righteous soul real living.

Here is if I live in righteous soul then, in the going up hard time then then this is righteous soul real living, but also hearing broadcasting from righteous soul living in destination place, but also going down then this is living of "poor & righteous soul" this is to be "righteous soul & nothing" living, so that this is so excitement, out of perfect wicked soul "revenge and break".

But if I live in wicked soul, then in the going up then, it must be "wicked soul me" try to find "easy living" then it must be stop going up, but also do not endure of hard living, it must be stop going up, but also going down then, "wicked soul me" reluctant going down, so that "wicked soul me" do not living in "nothing" to be keep getting during going down then "wicked soul me" still anger of going down, in the end "wicked soul me" do revenge and break include me and other. Then "wicked soul me' fall to the wicked soul living in destination place.

What is real living?

Righteous soul going up enlighten going down make "nothing" even reverse also same, going up is hard to go up, going down is some easy but in the real living is variable appeared being poor is going down then make "nothing" is real living.

The living of righteous soul, it never been keep excitement, sometimes gloomy the other time is hard but also it is very same of weather changing, it must be in the micro concept world, this is weather

Micro concept world, macro concept world all has going up, going down of same weather variation.

Righteous soul real living

Going up Going down

This is real living

Going up is enlighten

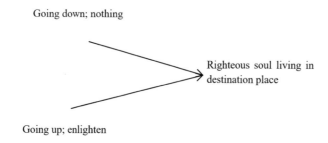

Going down; nothing

Righteous soul living in destination place

Going up; enlighten

This is righteous soul living runs to the righteous soul living in destination place.

Infer that to go righteous soul living in destination place, all macro concept world making true this process "the poor & righteous soul" and in the end "righteous soul & nothing" then safe returning to the righteous soul living in destination place.

Wicked soul living actor to be "easy living" does not living of "the poor & righteous soul" "righteous soul & nothing" then it must be the actor in the end of living being "revenge and break" by "wicked soul me".

In the macro concept world all out of me, but truly all from me, all of living is from me no other, this is true.

So that if do not living in righteous soul living then, wicked soul and mind level must be finished by "wicked soul me" include me and other as "revenge and break" strong energy.

So that righteous soul, real living is

Righteous soul living going up of hard time, being "enlighten" and suffer of loss of going down being "nothing" then, the way of "the poor & righteous soul" in the end "righteous soul & nothing" so that righteous soul living running to the righteous soul living in destination place, safe returning to the righteous soul living in destination place.

Righteous soul, real living is perfect safe from wicked soul living.

And living in righteous soul living in destination place, this is righteous soul, real living.

Righteous soul, real living

What is feeling of righteous soul? What feeling of real living.

Who knows "righteous soul me" real living

In book writing of righteous soul living is beginning of "mind=1/" then it start micro concept of living righteous soul meet me of body, so that righteous soul living, body is only shelter of righteous soul.

So then righteous soul me is righteous soul, but also body is shelter of righteous soul, so then it must be righteous soul living place, it is the same of righteous soul living in destination place.

Righteous soul me is righteous soul living in destination place.

Here is macro concept world, micro concept living destination is appeared to me, in me righteous soul living in destination place.

What is feeling of in me righteous soul living in destination place.

Here is it must be all of living of righteous soul living place, so that in this place living is "it shares time with other, help other, but also doing real love other'.

In the macro concept world, in this place all of living actors are living all has opportunity to be living in the micro concept world righteous soul living in destination place living.

But as the mind=1/, righteous soul living meet body, so then righteous soul manage body to live in the macro concept world but living is righteous soul living, so that righteous soul living actor of me feeling in "excitement".

Righteous soul in the micro concept world, dreamed to meet body then righteous soul meet real living place all of creatures, but also righteous soul will do righteous behavior with body, "it shares time with other, help other but also doing real love other".

As that "righteous soul Me" must be feeling in "excitement'.

Truly, living in me, just can do that righteous soul living behavior then, it must be "it shares time with other, help other, but also doing real love other" until now I feel that leaning through micro concept point, I heard before, righteous soul living behavior " JUST DO HELP AND DOING REAL LOVE" as activation of righteous soul, so that strong righteous soul move anytime any place, so that as while righteous soul me being " righteous soul & nothing" so that righteous soul me segregated from wicked soul, righteous soul me is just righteous soul, so that in the base of macro concept world, so body is righteous soul living in destination place, so in this macro concept world, "righteous soul Me" solve the problems of macro concept world, so all of problems is cause of mind level living actor "getting much more than others" but also wicked soul "using revenge and break power to live in easy living" this is problems, these problems all be solved through hearing broadcasting from righteous soul living in destination place.

As hearing broadcasting from righteous soul living in destination place, then now" righteous soul living me" do activate all of living righteous souls, helping from righteous soul living in destination place.

Righteous soul me do living righteous soul living and feeling excitement, this is first living in the macro concept world.

How to living is feeling in excitement, it must be keep strong righteous soul, then it must be body condition being the same of righteous soul living in destination place, so long, mind is 1/, righteous soul keep awaken, but also righteous soul living energy helped from righteous soul living in destination place.

Righteous soul me is keep micro concept point getting deeper place running, this is keep going to the destination place arrive is just living of righteous soul, to get energy because of the near to the righteous soul living in destination place.

Righteous soul living in destination place is deepest place, but also center of the all of the directions, but also the place energy is just like sun energy, so that righteous soul me keep running to the righteous soul living in destination place, then righteous soul of macro concept world base of righteous soul living me is doing "it shears time with other, help other, but also doing real love other" make possible.

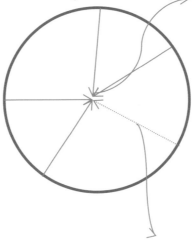

Righteous soul living in destination place

In the macro concept world righteous soul me, running ways

Righteous soul living in destination place

In the macro concept world righteous soul me, running ways

Righteous soul living in destination place is only deepest place micro concept king is "nothing" place is righteous soul living in destination place, righteous soul living actors are running to the righteous soul living in destination place.

Just righteous soul living dots are the ways to the righteous soul living in destination place. Whoever all can go to the righteous soul living in destination place?

If getting out of the dot point then the place is wicked soul living in destination place, wicked soul living actors are "revenge and break" so that all of wicked soul bans to go righteous soul's running to the righteous soul living in destination place.

So long, righteous soul living is awaken to keep running to the righteous soul living in destination place.

Righteous soul living is all the time being in the body, is form of the nothing, so that righteous soul living peace living, then peace living of righteous soul supplied to righteous soul me in excitement living.

Running to the righteous soul living

I say to me, "monk water" even now just saying to me, but truly living in righteous soul me must be living "monk water".

Water is from high to lower, somehow lowest, is same truth of knowledge "deepest" so that water is remaining position is the place of righteous soul living in destination place or base of righteous soul living actor.

Just keep running to the righteous soul living in destination place. The place is must "righteous soul & nothing".

Why righteous soul "me" living in this way, probably this enlighten is only me, because this is righteous soul me living, what can I do for other saying "righteous soul Me" living, but I will running to the righteous soul living in destination, this is real living, this is only what I can do living.

Righteous soul "me" can do anytime anyplace righteous soul me living "it shares time with other and help other, but also doing love others" on today I heard from righteous soul living in destination place, using righteous soul, righteous soul energy to transfer to the righteous soul living important living actors just like leaders all of leading to the place, then a leader is living in righteous soul living actor then the leader can lead all of living actors to the righteous soul living in destination place, so that in the micro concept point I will meet righteous souls of leaders, then righteous soul me, can do righteous soul behavior "it share time with other, help other, but also doing real love other".

Feeling righteous soul me, doing behavior of righteous soul me

Feeling righteous soul me, it must be I will be shares from a righteous souls, but also I will be helped from other righteous souls, but also doing real loved from other righteous souls.

Feeling righteous soul me is excitement, I want to be living in the righteous soul living in destination place, so that it must be feeling in peace and excitement is righteous soul living me feeling.

Righteous soul living behavior is

While keep running to the righteous soul living in destination place, but keep help other to know righteous soul living behavior, but also using righteous soul me, other righteous soul make strong, then other righteous soul will do their living for the righteous soul living place in peace and excitement.

From today, I will help other righteous soul to make peace and excitement living place in the macro concept world living place.

Righteous soul, real living

Living in clean clear in me is righteous soul real living?

Last night in the dream, I saw feeling in clean clear righteous soul me was living in the place of clean clear.

But also, living in righteous soul real living of clean clear is a huge energy of sun which is all burn of wicked soul.

Clean clear of righteous soul is sun of energy, all of thinking of wicked soul be possible fire all, so that the place making "nothing" so long the place and time occupied by righteous soul.

Clean clear of righteous soul is sun energy.

Clean clear of righteous soul living is excitement. Clean clear is just like sunset time feeling. This is in me, not a place of macro concept world righteous soul feeling in the shelter of righteous soul living.

This feeling was first to me, truly as living in righteous soul must learning time so that righteous soul living in destination place keep teaching me, so that it must be righteous soul me, educated from righteous soul living in destination place living prepared.

Truly righteous soul me understanding all of scripture of religious, so that I'm reading scripture, then it is the what I'm living is right or not, I can see before living of righteous soul living actors and me is what is difference then it is same.

Every time, place righteous soul living actor is living. The righteous soul is make the place clean clear, so that the place living actors are all do righteous soul behavior " it shares time with other, help other and doing real love other". The place is being bright by living of righteous soul living actor.

Clean clear of righteous soul of sun energy is really excitement to me, truly righteous soul me, hard to sleep after comeback from work place, the it comes to me feeling of lonesome, then I must be drop to the wicked soul, so that I need to find, then righteous soul living in destination place make me known to me " how about to buy radio" so then I directly buy radio, then I hear radio, so right after hear of radio is keep in righteous soul "me", the circumstance is same as before work place, so that righteous soul is being consistence, I feel excitement sleep, the in the dream I saw the clean clear of living in me.

But also in the place, righteous soul of real living in clean clear is the sun energy, righteous soul me is so excitement, if I live in righteous soul living, then sun of righteous soul living energy can fire all of "thinking of wicked soul and seed of wicked soul" so that righteous soul real living of clean clear sun energy is being "righteous soul & nothing".

Righteous soul real living is connected, in the macro concept world, then meeting by accident, then the place living also, righteous soul real living actor meeting.

Rare case I was experiment, to be cut my hair, I search hair dresser shop, then tree shops being possible cutting my hair, then the place was not by the road, but the place is in the apartment commercial building, truly righteous soul me like the place, the I drop in the shop then the hair dresser was old she said that 69 years old, then her behavior and talking was touch in mind, she lived like me trying to live righteous soul living.

After cutting my hair, righteous soul me, living in the shop talking righteous soul living. Her shop for 40 years; she said not to make money but help customers hair, so that now ding my age of 69 years old, but truly her hand is somewhat treble, but I was so excitement.

Rare case, hard to meet like her; so that I decide to go cut my hair, but also righteous soul living is touch in deep her saying, so righteous soul me feeling excitement.

Righteous soul real living of clean clear of sun energy, this is real living of excitement. Burn "thinking of wicked soul" then in me living is righteous soul, this is also get know today getting knowledge from righteous soul living in destination place.

Yesterday I get o knowledge; using righteous soul helping other to be peace in living, helping with righteous soul is macro concept world being righteous soul living in destination place making.

Today I got knowledge is "righteous soul real living of clean clear then the energy is like sun, this clean clear of energy make burn and fire "thinking of wicked soul and all root and seeds" then disappeared "thinking of wicked soul" then occupied by righteous soul, and this is real living of excitement.

Righteous soul, real living

Righteous soul real living is enlightened of macro concept world and micro concept world living, so that righteous soul living actor running to the righteous soul living in destination place of beginning of the micro concept world righteous soul living in destination place.

Righteous soul, real living is living and growth, this is so important.

Here is living and growth is righteous soul is growth also understanding, righteous soul is changed into from "the poor & righteous soul" and "righteous soul & nothing" this is growing, so that macro concept world feeling of righteous soul is being "nothing" this is righteous soul growing, "nothing" is righteous soul living place of living and eternity growth.

Macro concept world living actors of "mind level living actor" go old is getting much more than other, so that mind level living actors are safe by getting much more than others.

So that as mind=1/, then appeared to an actor righteous soul living is living, so that mind is feeling in the macro concept world then, there is no space righteous soul living feeling.

Somehow righteous soul living growth is must be also mins being decreasing process, so long in the end mind being 1/, micro concept point -1/~+1/, then in the end connect through micro concept point, then it beginning righteous soul living in the macro concept world.

Righteous soul real living is keep growing righteous soul connecting with righteous soul living in destination place; helping righteous soul running to the righteous soul living in destination, the all of obstacles being clear through getting knowledge, through micro concept point, so then that is called broadcasting from righteous soul living in destination place.

Righteous soul, real living is living and growth, this is so important

Living is growing

Righteous soul is living

Righteous soul growing

To grow righteous soul must be keeping mind=1/

Growing righteous soul, "the poor & righteous soul= child" but "righteous soul & nothing=adult"

Righteous soul of adult can do strong "it shares time with other, help other, but also doing real love other".

In the time of "the poor & righteous soul" living for distance wicked soul "revenge and break" but "righteous soul & nothing" is strong power of righteous soul who is sun of energy, righteous soul & nothing is clean clear living.

Clean clear of righteous soul is Sun energy, this energy burn "thinking of wicked soul' so that wick soul being clean clear by sun energy.

Clean clear of righteous soul is Sun energy

Is being living of righteous soul behavior of "it shares time with other, help other, but also doing real love other"

In the feeling of macro concept world righteous soul if do help other, righteous soul behavior is possible helping carry out.

Righteous soul sun energy is origin from righteous soul living and growth, all of energy micro concept point but the energy is huge in the macro concept world.

If righteous soul real living, then righteous soul behavior make possible, around of righteous soul living actor the place is righteous soul living in destination place. The place is peace and excitement is usual.

Righteous soul, real living

This book "righteous soul, real living" started as macro concept world me is "righteous soul me" what I am feeling living of righteous soul me?

If some condition is changed then righteous soul feeling is also changed, so sensitive soul living.

In me is a big change "week end living of work place begin of Monday night, but also returning to the home of Friday night is so changed time, then macro concept world living also suffering"

Righteous soul me of Monday night is feeling of unsafe and feeling lonesome, in this time wicked soul attack me temptation, then righteous soul living is moment disappeared time comes.

In this time, try to keep running to the righteous soul living in destination place, but righteous soul me losing from me, all of wicked soul is occupied me, so I'm sin, in this moment I'm sin.

Just moment all of philosophical value all ignorance, I'm strong wicked soul living actor, in my imagination then I am fully cross from righteous soul to wicked soul.

Just circumstance change is also affected righteous soul living also effected to live.

Righteous soul and lover is so important bride and bride groom living is balance is keep from wicked soul; this is righteous soul living running to the righteous soul living in destination place going so urgent critical living.

Family living is also fort living of righteous soul living.

Family must be living of righteous soul living.

In this family is must be living in righteous soul living behavior of "it shares time with family, help family and doing real love family" it is comes true without any explaining.

Righteous soul, real living

In the family mother father son and daughter all is living righteous soul living activation then, the family is also righteous soul living in destination place

Righteous soul me, righteous soul living then, the place of body is shelter of righteous soul of being righteous soul living in destination place, but today family is all of righteous soul living place of macro concept world righteous soul living in destination place.

Living in righteous soul is so sensitive so that macro concept world righteous soul real living is careful living, family living is not simple in the family, all of righteous souls are all living.

In the family, father righteous soul, mother righteous soul, righteous soul me, and son righteous soul, daughter righteous soul, then this is living of excitement living place, just like righteous soul living in destination place.

In the family is living of righteous soul living in destination place excitement living.

Hear family is all of righteous soul living feeling, so that righteous soul living is warm energy is make safe all family.

In this place wicked soul must not to be living, because family is righteous soul living in destination place, if a family wicked soul living actor is living then, the place never ever being righteous soul living in destination place.

Because righteous soul living in destination place is micro concept world living place segregated from wicked soul, wicked soul and righteous soul living is segregating.

But infer that in the family, macro concept world mind level living actor or wicked soul living actor and righteous soul living actor is mixed, so that an righteous soul living actor do living of righteous soul living behavior "it shares time with other, help other, but also doing real love other" then in the family keep progress righteous soul living actors.

Righteous soul, real living

Infer of oriental philosophy of "I Ching" then righteous soul living also going up and down, then righteous soul living also face to changing so that in the change so long, going up while running to the high place running is so hard, but just moment reach at top of high, then some after going down, while running down then in the end going down, in the end perfect lowest place reaching.

But also righteous soul run high so hard living but reach at the top of high then going down to the lowest place, this is righteous soul living, running to the righteous soul living, so then here is not known going up is hard going down is hard, but up and down is occur of righteous soul living actor

But while going up and down but the running is keeping to the righteous soul living in destination place, this is living.

But wicked soul living actor is wanted to keep in the place of high and top, not to be going down, all of energy used; wicked soul living energy is "revenge and break power" so that wicked soul living is make break, so then going down is not natural but mind and wicked soul's break all time and place, all of living actor are revenged in the end, all of wicked souls are disappeared in the same time of place.

Sorry to my reading book

Truly, righteous soul me is keep concerning based on "micro concept" so that righteous soul living actor appeared in the micro concept point "-1/~+1/ just micro concept world of "righteous soul and wicked soul" concerning is righteous soul me.

Infer that righteous soul living running is up and down living, this is all the time living, 1/righteous soul living is not flat but a slop is real living.

So why

In the family a living is to going up, the other is going down, but also an is middle of going high but also the other is down of middle all of running to the righteous soul living in destination place and time is not same, even a wicked soul is try to live in "easy living" an actor do not follow of up and down, then break the up and down, wicked soul is break of wicked soul energy up and down chain, then the living is all be disappeared from macro concept world, the urgent reach at the wicked soul living in destination place.

What is real living of righteous soul?

The poor & righteous soul and keep running to the righteous soul being "righteous soul & nothing" this running of righteous soul living in destination place.

"Righteous soul & nothing" this is must be feeling in the macro concept world righteous soul me

"Righteous soul & nothing" feeling righteous soul me running to the feeling of righteous soul & nothing, this is living of righteous soul me, real living, righteous soul real living is this.

Righteous soul, real living

Feeling of righteous soul, real living on "the poor & righteous soul"

Macro concept world righteous soul me real living of "the poor& righteous soul"

Righteous soul me righteous soul living declare

Righteous soul me do not fear of poor living

Righteous soul me do not have anything

This is real living of mind=1/

Righteous soul living is running to the righteous soul living in destination place.

So then mind governing body is free from mind lie that is all of living is only macro concept world, there is no micro concept world.

Truly righteous soul knows that there is micro concept world.

Righteous soul of real living is macro concept world and micro concept world both world living.

So that righteous soul living actor know that macro micro living of righteous soul living, for this free from mind lie, so that mind=1/

Then it comes real living of righteous soul

Righteous soul me do not fear of poor living

Righteous soul me do not have anything

Even macro concept world living also important but this is macro concept world living only, so then it require of balance both macro concept world and micro concept world living going.

Righteous soul living of real living is running to the righteous soul living in destination place, so that righteous soul real living is "the poor & righteous soul" truly I didn't know that real living of the poor & righteous soul.

This is truly free from poor living fear.

But righteous soul of real living is beyond of mind level living.

So righteous soul "me" declare

Righteous soul me do not fear of poor living

Righteous soul me do not have anything

Righteous soul living actor runs like water to the righteous soul living in destination place, righteous soul living running is to the lowest place, just like water end remaining place.

"The poor & righteous soul" this is really excitement living.

Do not know this righteous soul living, so that my living of macro concept world relatives are must be living wealth, so then normal living of it must use them, this is real living of macro concept world.

If retied from macro concept world living, then it must be free from mind level rule living, so that righteous soul "me" real living is being beginning "the poor & righteous soul living"

What I am living is "the poor & righteous soul"

Make me righteous soul; make clean clear in me; all of mind residue all be burnt and cleaned is based on living, this is "the poor & righteous soul".

As not clean clear of mind then nothing of "poor" if this then, this is son of beach living.

What I will living is " the poor & righteous soul" this is independent from deceit mind, so then mind must be being "nothing" so that in me the poor in me, is all occupied by righteous soul.

This is so excitement living because righteous soul is running fast to the righteous soul living in destination place, because there is no obstacle running to the righteous soul living in destination place.

"the poor & righteous soul" is healthy and strong righteous soul running fast to the righteous soul living in destination place, so that righteous soul "me" living in excitement as " the poor & righteous soul" perfect out of mind level living,

Even all the time of living but all the time mind level living and righteous soul living is mixed, so that try to live of righteous soul real living but there is no possible, but after retired then, it must me righteous soul "me" feeling so excitement without mind deceit.

So I'm again declare of living "the poor & righteous soul"

Righteous soul me do not fear of poor living

Righteous soul me do not have anything

Righteous soul, real living

Righteous soul is in me, who is watch wicked soul behavior.

Righteous soul so hard to live seeing wicked soul behavior but also wicked soul keep try to make righteous soul disappear from me, so that wicked soul to get all of me, so called being wicked soul me.

Truly righteous soul me is so fear "thinking of wicked soul" thinking of wicked soul produce "lonesome, fear, hate, of revenge and break" so that just righteous soul even awaken then, righteous soul do not to be deceit from wicked soul, then it must be righteous soul always be awaken.

Truly righteous souls me feel in "lonesome" in the dormitory after day working, then righteous soul stumble down of body tired, then moment it comes to me, thinking of wicked soul of "lonesome" then to be sleep, I followed to the wicked soul, so that I got a sin.

truly I love my wife who makes me philosopher, truly she is my bodhisattva who already righteous soul living actor, in her is righteous soul living actor, she make me living in righteous soul living.

It very recently it comes to me, what I hear of "the poor & righteous soul" then I wrote book, but until now I do not know, how to live in macro concept world is "righteous soul, real living" but I hear of broadcasting from righteous soul living in destination place.

Then after hear broadcasting from righteous soul, righteous soul me create me "I will not fear of poor living, I will not get my own" this is righteous soul real living.

"I will not fear of poor living, I will not get my own"

This is make me free from macro concept world "mind level living"

Truly going with body, then mind level living is followed with righteous soul me, all of macro concept world constructed as the mine level living.

So then, I was cling to the mind level living of safe living of getting my own and fear being poor" this is mind level living actor of righteous soul living actor feeling in macro concept world.

At last I feel "do not fear of poor, but also do not have my own" this will be occupied in righteous soul me,

Righteous soul me id free from mind level unclean in me,

Righteous soul me, real living of clean clear is real living. That is free from wicked soul living of cloudy in me.

"Do not fear of poor, but also do not have my own"

All of righteous soul living actors had lived, so that just only one time of valuable living, they independent from mind level false living, but also wicked soul living of "revenge and break" energy.

Truly righteous soul real living

This is feeling in the micro concept world, weather condition "being clean clear" this is righteous soul real living.

This is real living of excitement living but also through micro concept world get creation of knowledge to run to the righteous soul living in destination place.

Not to be lost way to the righteous soul living in destination place, righteous soul living actor, keep hear broadcasting from righteous soul living in destination place, but also get creature of knowledge, then this is all survive same place living wicked soul living.

The only way to being independent from wicked soul living "revenge and break" then it must be being "righteous soul & nothing", so righteous soul living "there is no righteous soul "nothing" then it comes wicked soul also being "nothing"

Righteous soul living of free from wicked soul "revenge and break" then righteous soul living is also hard to live, but also in the macro concept world living hard living from wicked soul, but survive then, in the end of safe reaching righteous soul living in destination place living of righteous soul living behavior "it shares time with other, help other, but also doing real love other"

Righteous soul living behavior "it shares time with other, help other, and doing real love other"

This is all enlighten from macro concept world living, so that the being of "righteous soul & nothing" safe returning to the righteous soul living in destination place.

That kind of living actor of righteous soul living actors are returning from righteous soul living in destination place, in the place, righteous soul me, reach at then, righteous soul & nothing, just excitement eternity do living of righteous soul living behavior " it shares time with other, help other, but also doing real love other'.

Truly, macro concept world it must be living and learning with body, then after out of body in the living of righteous soul living in destination place all living is righteous soul real living.

Out of wicked soul living, the place is righteous soul living in destination place, the place all living actor is righteous souls living in eternity.

Righteous soul, real living

Righteous soul and wicked soul is compared with

Righteous soul is clean body; clean dirty on body

Wicked soul is dirty on body

Truly living in the macro concept world can live

Righteous soul of clean body or wicked soul dirty body living can possible, so that just one time living in the macro concept world, no one knows how serious living now in the macro concept world.

Truly it may possible dirty of wicked soul, or clean of righteous soul, but cleaning is body is macro concept world, then in this macro concept world do not clean body of living of wicked soul, then it will be the time soon passed, so that losing opportunity making body clean living of righteous soul living.

Then losing cleaning body of righteous soul living, then the wicked soul living actor repent after living macro concept world, at now living of macro concept world living in a time and place, all of wicked soul, and mind level living actor, but also righteous soul living all of living actors are living.

But macro to micro, so that in the micro concept world, living is soul living is real living so that, the micro concept world segregated wicked soul living in destination place, and righteous soul living in destination place.

Until book writing, righteous soul, and wicked soul, the circumstance, I did not know, but today, I heard broadcasting from righteous soul living in destination place and wicked soul living in destination place.

Righteous soul is clean body; clean dirty on body

Wicked soul is dirty on body

In the macro concept world symbol of wicked soul is dirty on body, and then righteous soul is clean body.

In the micro concept world living of wicked soul living in destination place living circumstance must be infer of dirty place.

But in the micro concept world living place of righteous soul living in destination place is must be infer of clean place.

Wicked soul living actor living place dirty living circumstance

Righteous soul living actor living place clean living circumstance

This is here is understand of mind level living actor, so that dirty and clean is usual, but living of righteous soul living is clean clear in micro concept world living, so that the place, connect or micro concept point to connect between macro concept world righteous soul and micro concept world righteous soul.

Here is clean soul of righteous soul connecting or micro concept point is clean clear of sunshine place, but also righteous soul is also bright and so that in the time and place of "-1/~+1/" between the time and pace meet both macro concept world righteous soul, micro concept world righteous soul.

This is real living of righteous soul living, who living in the macro concept world through micro concept point, hear broadcasting righteous soul living creative information of knowledge safe returning to the righteous soul living in destination place, because micro concept world righteous soul living in destination living place excitement living, so that righteous soul living behavior of "it shares time with other, help other, but also doing real love other"

Wicked soul living dirty place

Wicked soul living of macro concept world then, the wicked soul "easy living" in the macro concept world, the place was clean using getting wicked soul power of "revenge and break" then, the easy living of wicked soul run to the place someplace, but wicked soul living actor do not know in the macro concept world, all of energy used up to live in "easy living" so that there is no energy to clean body and then being living of " it shares time with other, help other, but also doing real love other" then the time of macro concept world lived of dirty in body of wicked soul living.

Easy living of wicked soul anger

I cleaned body every day, why I'm now in dirty place of wicked soul, truly, infer that that is righteous, here is body is opportunity to get changed from wicked soul to righteous soul living, because in the micro concept world of living in the place of wick soul hard to live dirty place, so that wicked soul run out from micro concept world difficult opportunity to "revenge and break" of long time wicked soul living dirty place living, so then wicked soul, just with body, keep living in "easy living" so keep cycle because in the macro concept world "easy living" is better than "the poor & righteous soul" in the macro concept world, only seen to the wicked soul "poor" because macro concept world do not see, "the poor & righteous soul" but to the righteous soul living do not see "the poor" but see only "righteous soul".

Easy living of wicked soul anger, anger of wicked soul do not know

In the macro concept world, righteous soul living actor all of living time is "it shares time with other, help other, but also doing real love other".

So that living all of suffer of running to the righteous soul living in destination place, so that suffer time how to solve the suffer of problems, then all of solving methods, before living saints writing book reading, and attend the church and Buddha temple, so that while growing and as the mind=1/, the being enlighten of it appear of righteous soul meeting, so then it keep living of righteous soul me.

Probably righteous soul me same as the macro concept world wicked soul, mind level, but now righteous soul me is comes from as the all of suffering peak of suffering, in moment being "mind-1/, so that now feel of righteous soul living.

What is righteous soul living feeling?

"Righteous soul "me" keep watch thinking of wicked soul"

"Righteous soul "me" living watch thinking of wicked soul, but also righteous soul "me" hearing broadcasting from righteous soul living in destination place"

Until now no one read book 9 books are based on hearing broadcasting from righteous soul living in destination place, just righteous soul "me" safe running to the righteous soul living in destination place.

Today I heard

Righteous soul is clean body; clean dirty on body

Wicked soul is dirty on body

Macro concept world is all open for chance to live righteous soul living.

Today saying the ways

Wicked soul living actor if clean body then living clean, clean living is same as clean living of righteous soul living.

As soon as possible, the half wicked soul, half righteous soul, then strong righteous soul behavior "it shares time with other, help other, but also doing real love other'

So that as cleaning wicked soul must be loved from lover of righteous soul, who is saver of wicked soul, so then, righteous soul mission carried, what is mission of righteous soul from righteous soul living in destination place with tool of righteous soul living " doing real love other" so that righteous soul meet lover who is now cleaning wicked soul, then righteous soul do strong real love cleaning wicked soul, so then righteous soul mission carry then righteous soul do complete mission, then mission clear.

Righteous soul "me" now do mission, cleaning body of my lover is living with me, so then to complete of mission clear, righteous soul "me" so huge hard living, "it shares time with her, and help her, and doing real love her" at now I'm living for the purpose to make mission clear.

This is righteous soul, real living.

Righteous soul, real living

Righteous soul in the macro concept world now traveling, from micro concept world to macro concept world, micro concept world meet wicked soul, macro concept world meet lover of wicked soul, righteous soul living keep living with wicked soul in the both world,

So that righteous soul living is facing of wicked soul "revenge and breaking energy".

Righteous soul, real living

This is from micro world to macro world living is real living.

Righteous soul feel macro concept world and micro concept world is round. Righteous soul living is voyage micro concept world righteous soul living, macro concept world righteous soul living actor with body; righteous soul living actor meet through micro concept point (-1/~+1/)

Righteous soul living

Micro concept world voyage meet wicked soul who assert equality between wicked soul and righteous soul to travel macro concept world, so that righteous soul traveled in micro concept world.

Righteous soul living with wicked soul how feels in the macro concept world?

In the body shelter both righteous soul and wicked soul living.

Keep meet body, both righteous soul, and wicked soul with body mission carry so that

Righteous soul with body mission is

Do real love lover and make lover righteous soul, keep running to the righteous soul living in destination place.

Wicked soul with body mission is

Do "revenge and break" righteous soul, wicked soul, mind level living actor, even shelter of body; wicked soul living actor so anger in the living wicked soul living in destination place of dirty place.

Righteous soul living actor mission

Wicked soul living actor mission

Against energy

In the actor of body, both righteous souls, wicked soul is equal then the actor must be energy power balance so that still peace even righteous soul living actor feels fear of wicked soul energy.

This is balance between righteous soul energy and wicked soul energy is young time it must be because youth are do not know, still young, poor in knowledge as getting ages.

But righteous soul move to mission carry out

"Meet lover, and make lover righteous soul, keep running with lover to the righteous soul living in destination place"

The same as wicked soul move to mission carry out

"Revenge and break others"

Righteous soul living actor runs to the righteous soul living in destination place, but wicked soul dead of righteous soul so that wicked soul runs to the wicked soul living in destination place.

Here is dead means righteous soul living actor disappeared cause of wicked soul "revenge and break', then this righteous soul do not safe returning to the righteous soul living in destination place.

In the micro concept world

Righteous soul just watch "thinking of wicked soul" just thinking is disappeared then righteous soul feeling "clean clear", truly "thinking of wicked soul" is in the micro concept world "windy, cloudy, anger lonesome etc."

As the same

Macro concept world

Righteous soul living actor only do "real love wicked soul" but the same as micro concept world, just watch is righteous soul living actor safe living to run righteous soul living in destination place.

Micro concept world is not recognition

So that even all governing, but all ignorance because most macro concept world living actors are wicked soul, mind level living actors.

But macro concept world righteous soul living actor

Just keep give righteous soul living energy, this is only survived from wicked soul, but also safe running to the righteous soul living in destination place.

Righteous soul me

To survive and do mission carry out

I said to my righteous soul "righteous soul help me righteous soul; still small righteous soul under the heavy rock of wicked soul, so that righteous soul me, to grow give righteous soul living energy, but also help best condition to live righteous soul living.

Truly in real living of macro concept world

So that righteous soul me keep saying righteous soul me righteous soul, "righteous soul go righteous soul and help and give energy" after then keep watch macro concept world then, truly appear up of righteous soul living behavior; this is the role of righteous soul living actor doing.

Truly in the macro concept world

If I be strong righteous soul "me" then wicked soul also "strong wicked soul" match up with righteous soul, so in the real living of righteous soul living, lover is over the normal wicked soul, but also I'm strong righteous soul, so that keep help lover of righteous soul, I must be save from strong wicked soul of lover, that is living in the macro concept world real living.

Righteous soul "me" is also being "righteous soul living actor" so that righteous soul living actor me, keep help to be righteous soul living actor, but also keep with running to the righteous soul living in destination place.

This is so dangerous living, because string wicked soul keep help my wicked soul, so then possible righteous soul me disappeared cause of wicked soul lover, so that the same as micro concept world "thinking of wicked soul" just watch, the same as I'm doing real love lover to be righteous soul living, but do not get in to wicked soul, then it must be righteous soul me, wicked soul get energy, so that righteous soul me, keep watching and doing real love lover.

As living righteous soul, real living is

Even fear of wicked soul, but righteous soul living actor mission is "making lover righteous soul, and running to the righteous soul living in destination safe comeback" this is righteous soul living real living of macro concept world living place.

What is righteous soul, real living?

Righteous soul is passenger

Real living is getting on train for Righteous soul living in destination place.

In this living way, then in the moment, it comes to "righteous soul me" then passenger decision is wrong, so that wicked soul "revenge and break" so that "righteous soul me" getting for righteous soul living in destination place.

Why it possible?

So urgent important running to the righteous soul living in destination place going, but it get down train, the righteous soul being disappeared from moving to righteous soul living in destination place.

Living in macro concept world of righteous soul living; same living of righteous soul living "it shares time with other, help other, but also doing real love other"

The poor & righteous soul, righteous soul & nothing of righteous soul, but if still has righteous soul, anti-pair of wicked soul still living.

Wicked soul of "easy living" and righteous soul of poor living, then if righteous soul living sleeping then, it invader of righteous soul by wicked soul, then in a moment, righteous soul being disappeared in me, then righteous soul changed into wicked soul, so all of running to the righteous soul living is stop.

It is fully possible?

Right before I got a temptation from wicked soul of "easy living"

But truly easy living, there is no excitement to me, then it must be come back righteous soul me.

Even hard living but if I living as righteous soul living then, it must be so excitement, because it has direction to go for, but wicked soul easy living is anything direction, so that any way going is possible, then there is not going but remained in block to the future, this is not living in excitement.

So then living in righteous soul living is keep running to the righteous soul living in destination place, this is "it shares time with other, help other, but also doing real love other"

In the time of all of actors are calling then helping pray but also do real love in the pray, so this is righteous soul living behavior.

But also righteous soul living actor help other, some of income is not mine but other, this is symbol of what I'm living in righteous soul me or not, so truly, helping is not mare but this is secure of me my living in righteous soul living, so that on today my writing is on the way to the righteous soul living, being temptation from wicked soul living "easy living'.

As help my income to help other, then, hard living for one month, but as doing righteous soul living feeing in excitement, this is true my living, but I overcome of easy living temptation, so then righteous soul me is so feeling in excitement.

Righteous soul real living

Sure of righteous soul" me" is doing not fear of poor living

And righteous soul" me" do not my own.

This is so hard living expected, but truly other righteous soul also helping me, so that living in righteous soul is done, this is miracle to me; this is righteous soul, real living.

It maybe someone; who is not living in righteous soul whether who is righteous soul, wicked soul, mind level living actor, then saving money for safe is better, do not save helping other, then regard to me, "you are wrong" but righteous soul living is do not save but shares with other, help other, and doing real love other.

Truly last night, my asset was defunct so that I get loan from bank, then I paid loan money to other. Then moment I got a lost living in righteous soul living, save money for my "easy living" then I'm being wicked soul living actor.

Soon after turn back to the righteous soul living, I do not save money but keep routine helping other who is really needed righteous soul me, this is keep me strong depending attacking from wicked souls.

Keep living in righteous soul living is required to me to go for the righteous soul living in destination place.

Righteous soul, real living

Righteous soul living with "thinking of wicked soul"

Righteous soul living actor wants to living as "righteous soul & nothing" but "thinking of wicked soul" keep bounce up to the critical line of righteous soul, so then righteous soul watching it.

Righteous soul sometimes lost running to the righteous soul living in destination place, then the time and space all occupied by "thinking of wicked soul"

Righteous soul living; creating knowledge helping righteous soul running to the righteous soul living in destination place, this is feeling of macro concept world righteous soul is "clean clear".

Thinking of wicked soul; fear, lonesome, revenge and break etc. all attacking "me" so then, thinking of wicked soul living in the past, this is not helping out of past, just living "easy living" of past living.

Righteous soul, real living

If righteous soul living then nearby also living wicked soul living.

This is organism of living. This is mixed then who all do not know exist of righteous soul, wicked soul, mind level living.

But macro concept world; mind level of not true with body, but from micro concept world wicked soul, and righteous soul living place

Micro concept world; without mind, just righteous soul world, wicked soul world is segregate.

So called soul living place must be infer that three place

Macro concept world one, micro concept world wicked soul living place one, righteous soul living place one, but truly two, because

Micro concept world righteous soul living in destination only one is recognition, but wicked soul living in destination place is one recognition, so that micro wicked to macro world, micro righteous soul to macro world is so then it must be two.

Righteous soul, real living

Living in the macro concept world, so many variable conditions are unfold to the living of macro concept world me, every second happening events are must be 1/

Righteous soul living is in the micro concept world living place

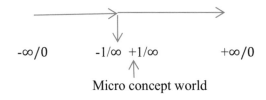

$-\infty/0$ $-1/\infty$ $+1/\infty$ $+\infty/0$

Micro concept world

Living is now time and space this is righteous soul real living, this is micro concept world living (-1/~+1/) this is beyond from past, so that in this place there is no "thinking of wicked soul"

If righteous soul living is sleeping then drop into "thinking of wicked soul" so that righteous soul keep watching "thinking of wicked soul", just righteous soul is safe living place "-1/~+1/" only in in this time and space is volcano of larva, so called fluid "creature of knowledge" coming up. Safe living from "thinking of wicked soul" is

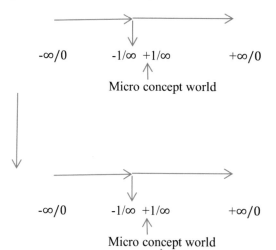

−∞/0   −1/∞   +1/∞   +∞/0

Micro concept world

Running to the righteous soul living in destination place

−∞/0   −1/∞   +1/∞   +∞/0

Micro concept world

−∞/0   −1/∞   +1/∞   +∞/0

Micro concept world

Righteous soul living in destination place

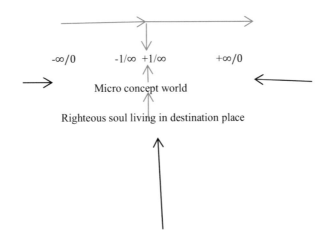

Righteous soul living actor living in the micro concept point is running to the righteous soul living in destination place.

If righteous soul do not living in micro concept point, then the living is in the past living of wicked soul, all of living with "thinking of wicked soul".

What is righteous soul, real living?

Righteous soul, real living is micro concept point

This is -1/~+1/, in this time and space righteous soul living is possible.

In this time and space is segregated from "thinking of wicked soul"

Macro concept world feeling of righteous soul of "clean clear" this is out of "thinking of wicked soul"

Righteous soul, real living

Micro concept point (-1/ ~ +1/ is righteous soul moving line, so then micro concept point micro concept point, this is righteous soul move road, true this road to meet other righteous souls, so then most macro concept world living actors are all has micro concept point.

So long righteous soul living actor in the micro concept point, creature of knowledge is same hear broadcasting from righteous soul living in destination place.

So long, if righteous soul me living in righteous soul, then the place righteous soul micro concept are connect, so spread all of the righteous soul, so just do "righteous soul me" living in righteous soul living behavior "it shares time with other, help other, and doing real love other" then, truly righteous soul me is just corner of village where do not know other, then even automatically spread just in a second all of righteous soul living actor know.

Righteous soul, real living

It must know righteous soul to be "nothing" then still the place wicked soul also there, out of fear from wicked soul, what is first disappeared is "righteous soul", "righteous soul me" is being "nothing" then free from wicked soul.

Even not to be in "nothing" but keep running to the righteous soul living in destination place then, living in the righteous soul living in destination place, it must living in the micro concept point, it must be righteous soul must be being "nothing" then there is no wicked soul, so called " righteous soul & nothing" being.

In the macro concept world "righteous soul me" what feeling?

That is feeling in "excitement" without wicked soul, without "thinking of wicked soul" just pure living with "righteous soul & nothing".